MW01635651

body & beauty FOODS

body & beauty FOODS

OVER 100 DELICIOUS RECIPES TO IMPROVE YOUR HEALTH, INCREASE YOUR ENERGY AND ENHANCE YOUR LOOKS

HAZEL COURTENEY & KATHRYN MARSDEN

RECIPES CREATED BY ANNE SHEASBY

PUBLISHED BY THE READER'S DIGEST ASSOCIATION LIMITED
LONDON • NEW YORK • SYDNEY • CAPE TOWN • MONTREAL

A READER'S DIGEST BOOK

First published in Australia in 1998
by Reader's Digest (Australia) Pty Limited
26–32 Waterloo Street, Surry Hills, NSW 2010

Designed and produced by
THE IVY PRESS LIMITED
Lewes, East Sussex
BN7 1UP

National Library of Australia Cataloguing-in-Publication data
Courteney, Hazel.

Body & beauty foods: over 100 delicious recipes to improve your health, increase your energy and enhance your looks.

Includes index.
ISBN 0 86449 336 3.

1. Natural foods. 2. Diet therapy. 3. Health. I. Marsden, Kathryn. II. Reader's Digest (Australia). III. Title.

613.26

Art Director: *Peter Bridgewater*
Editorial Director: *Sophie Collins*
Managing Editor: *Anne Townley*
Commissioning Editor: *Viv Croot*
Designer: *Clare Barber*
Project Editor: *Caroline Earle*
Editor: *Molly Perham*
Photography: *Marie-Louise Avery*

Printed and bound in China

'Let food be your medicine and medicine be your food.'

HIPPOCRATES C.469–399 BC

foreword

Most people recognise that we are what we eat. But many do not realise that by choosing the right foods, we can change the way we look and feel – both inside and out. This book clearly explains which foods are most beneficial, for what purpose and why. It identifies foods that encourage beautiful skin, hair, nails and eyes, and foods that help boost our immune system, maintain strong teeth and bones, and lead to more flexible joints and a healthier heart.

During the past 50 years our diets and lifestyles have changed more radically than in the previous 2,000 years. Stress, pollution, pesticides, the overuse of antibiotics and other prescription drugs, plus the huge increase in fast foods, contribute to many health problems. But nutritional scientists and doctors now know that what we eat plays a role in many chronic conditions, such as arthritis, eczema, high blood pressure, cancer and heart disease.

Many of the foods we eat consist of highly refined, mass-produced, prepackaged and canned foods that often contain excessive amounts of salt, sugar and chemical additives, such as preservatives and flavourings – some of which are now known to cause aggression, hyperactivity and mood swings.

Unfortunately, many people talk about healthy eating but in reality continue to eat poorly. Eventually this causes a deficiency in vital nutrients and overloads the system with toxins, and we become ill. Body & Beauty Foods *helps to tip the scales in the direction of better health. The body can often heal itself if given the right tools for the job. Chosen with care to provide all the nutrients we need, food makes potent medicine.*

We all have the freedom to choose what we put in our mouths, and if you want to become and stay healthier you need to make the right choices. If you are reading these words you have already made a positive choice.

HAZEL COURTENEY

contents

foreword
5

introduction
8

what are body and beauty foods and how do they work?
12

notes on ingredients
18

notes on the recipes
19

basic recipes
20

body foods
22

immunity foods
24

heart and circulation foods
46

foods for teeth and bones
68

flexibility foods
86

beauty foods
104

fresh start
106

shape foods
118

skin and nail foods
136

hair foods
152

vision foods
168

which body problem needs which food?
186

which beauty problem needs which food?
187

vitamins and minerals chart
188

index
191

acknowledgements
192

introduction

Aim to eat at least five portions of fruit and vegetables a day for optimum nutrition.

The secret of a healthy diet is to forget the word 'dieting'. In fact, variety and balance are the keys to a lifetime of healthier eating. In this book Kathryn and I have selected many nutritious foods to help redress any imbalance in your diet using foods that heal rather than foods that harm. But don't panic – you can still enjoy your favourite treats. I'm sure you have heard the saying 'a little of what you fancy does you good' – but note the word little! When you eat something naughty, really enjoy it and don't feel guilty, but remember: balance in all things and keep refined, sugary, fatty meals and treats to a minimum. It's hard, I know, because we are regularly bombarded with advertising that encourages us to eat more of the latest snack bar, or prepackaged meal or fad drink – but these mass-produced foods and drinks may not have adequate nutritional value. If your diet contains more junk foods than healthy foods, you will be missing out on many vital nutrients.

Many people don't fully appreciate how diet can contribute to their health, and I explain that it is often a cumulative effect that triggers health problems. In most cases, it is not our last meal that makes us ill, but our last thousand. Allergy sufferers are painfully aware of how eating the wrong foods can affect their health, but we all need to remember that the right food is like a medicine, and that a balanced, varied diet is one of the simplest ways to better health.

To survive, the human body needs many nutrients, including vitamins, minerals, amino acids and essential fatty acids, plus air, water and light. Our bodies cannot manufacture these substances; we must obtain them from external sources. For good health, we need to eat sufficient quantities of high quality, fresh, unrefined whole foods. Because many fruits and vegetables are flown thousands of kilometres to reach our table and, once harvested, can lose up to 50 per cent of their vitamin content in just 10 days, we recommend that you eat locally grown, seasonal, preferably organic foods whenever possible.

Our health depends not only on what we eat, but also on our body's ability to absorb nutrients within the gut. Many people over 40 have digestive problems, often induced by stress and over-consumption of junk foods eaten in a hurry. One secret to improving absorption is to chew food more thoroughly, and to eat a little fresh pineapple, papaya or pawpaw, which contain digestive enzymes, with main meals. Or you can take a digestive enzyme tablet – these are available from all good health food stores.

Vitamins, minerals and essential fats from our food work synergistically (together) within the body, so you derive greater benefits from eating a variety of whole foods than from taking vitamin pills in isolation. An alfalfa sprout sandwich, for example, contains more nutrients than a cheap multi-vitamin tablet. Our bodies consist of approximately 63 per cent water, 22 per cent protein, 13 per cent fat and 2 per cent vitamins and minerals, and for optimum health we need to eat a balance of all the main food types – carbohydrates, proteins and fats.

The best source of energy is unrefined carbohydrates, since they release their natural sugars more slowly than highly refined foods such as mass-produced cakes and biscuits. For optimum health, 60 to 70 per cent of your diet should consist of unrefined, fibre-rich carbohydrates, which will help to raise your energy level and encourage the elimination of toxins. These carbohydrates include wholegrains, such as brown rice, millet, rye, unrefined wholewheat cereals, breads, pasta and pulses, and whole foods, such as vegetables and fruits. Sugar is a carbohydrate, however, after giving an initial energy burst, it can actually deplete your energy level. We have suggested a few healthier alternatives, but they are still forms of sugar and should be used in moderation. It is worth noting that the foods you crave most, such as saturated fats, sugar, caffeine and alcohol, often contribute to many health problems. Also, many foods labelled 'low fat' in fact have a high sugar content, and sugar in excess converts to fat in the body if it is not burned up during exercise. So read labels carefully!

Proteins are essential for muscle tone and growth, healthy skin and nails, for tissue repair and in the manufacture of hormones. They should make up 15–20 per cent of your daily diet. Vegetable-based proteins, such as lentils, kidney beans, soya bean curd, haricot beans, peas, corn, broccoli, runner beans and nuts (Brazil nuts, almonds, walnuts and pecan nuts are proteins), are preferable to animal-based proteins, as they are low in saturated (hard) fats and high in fibre. But again, as balance and variety are important, if you are not a vegetarian you can also enjoy fresh fish, eggs and chicken, and a little meat (preferably organic).

There is a great deal of misunderstanding regarding fats; many people believe that a healthy diet is one very low in fat, but this is not so. We all need a certain amount of fat, but it is the type of fat that is important. There are two kinds of fats: saturated and unsaturated. Saturated fats are the unhealthier fats, found mainly in meat and dairy products, and these are linked to hardening of the arteries and most major diseases. Unsaturated fats are the healthier fats, found in nuts, seeds and oily fish. Unsaturated fats fall into two types: monounsaturated fats are found in olive oil and avocados; polyunsaturated fats are found in nuts and seeds. For optimum health a sufficient intake of certain polyunsaturated fats known as essential fats because they are needed by every cell in the body to function properly. A lack of essential fats is linked to dry skin, eczema, psoriasis, water retention, hyperactivity, mood swings and difficulty in losing weight. Essential fats are found in seeds, such as sunflower, sesame and pumpkin seeds and linseeds, in their unrefined oils, and also in oily fish. Essential fats are easily destroyed by heating and by exposure to oxygen, so store salad dressings in the fridge. Many processed foods, such as cakes, pies, sausages, margarines and hamburgers, contain hydrogenated or 'trans' fats, which should be avoided as much as possible. Although butter is a saturated fat, Kathryn and I prefer butter when baking as it does not turn rancid when heated and is rich in vitamin A. Fat, mainly in the form of essential fats, should make up about 20–25 per cent of your daily diet.

Fruits and vegetables are packed with nutrients and fibre. Try to eat five types every day. Drink plenty of water, avoid excessive use of sodium-based salt, and take some exercise every day, even if it's only a relaxing walk. If we could all do this there would be a substantial decrease in heart disease, high blood pressure and degenerative conditions – even in the most ardent carnivores.

Remember that your body is capable of healing itself when given the right tools for the job. Every 72 hours your gut lining is completely replaced; every month your skin is renewed, every two years you manufacture a new skeleton and a new liver. The body strives to maintain a healthy balance, and our aim in this book is to help you to discover your own balance through a great variety of delicious recipes.

Fresh vegetables and wholegrains are packed with nutrients that will improve your looks and boost your energy level.

what are body *and* beauty foods *and* how do they work?

THE OLD SAYING 'you are what you eat' is absolutely right. Food is our source of energy. It also has the power to heal and to make us look more beautiful. The properties of certain foods have been known for generations, and modern science has uncovered the reasons why many tried and trusted recipes work. Research has also shown which other foods can positively enhance health, vitality and appearance. By choosing meals carefully, we can give our bodies a boost every day. All the foods listed here, as well as the delicious recipes that follow are packed with nutritional gems. Read on and discover the best body and beauty foods!

Fruit

apples

- Apples protect the heart. They are recommended to anyone with high blood cholesterol or blood glucose problems. Grated or mashed apple is an old remedy for diarrhoea. For weight watchers, apples are good to eat just before meals, as they blunt the appetite, and as a between-meal snack.
- Fibre. A medium-sized apple provides 15 per cent of the daily recommendation for fibre. Some of this is soluble fibre, which may help lower blood cholesterol.
- Pectin. Apples are rich in the soluble fibre pectin. Eating two apples a day pushes enough pectin through the blood to make a real dent in cholesterol levels for some people.
- Rich in vitamin C, plus worthwhile amounts of vitamin E.

apricots

- Beta carotene. Good for eyes, bones and teeth; helps boost immune function.
- Flavonoids. Apricots contain flavonoids, which strengthen capillaries, reducing the risk of bleeding and bruising. Deficiency signs are similar to those of vitamin C.
- Vitamin C. Used in the manufacture of collagen, the 'glue' that gives skin its elasticity and support. Vital for wound healing and resistance to infection. Common signs of low vitamin C intake are bleeding gums, thread veins and slow wound healing.

avocados

- An excellent skin food, both eaten and applied to the skin. Sadly avoided by many people because they are seen as a high-energy, fattening food, avocados should be classed with the 'healthy fats' and included more often in the diet.
- Monounsaturates (as in olive oil) and vitamin E.

bananas

- Pectin. Bananas have a higher pectin content even than apples. They are sweet, filling, sustaining, and easy to digest. Bananas are a good food for anyone who suffers from acid indigestion, reflux or ulcers, and are a good 'settling' food after stomach upset, or during recovery from food poisoning. Super-gentle fibre.
- Magnesium. Works with essential fatty acids, calcium and the B group vitamins to support the nervous system and maintain healthy cell production.
- Vitamins C and B_6, folate, pectin, potassium.

blackberries

- Calcium and magnesium. Blackberries are especially rich in these, so are a good food for the bones.
- Vitamin C. 300g/11oz of blackberries provides half the recommended daily intake.

blackcurrants

- Antioxidants and B group vitamins. Essential for healthy eyes.
- Flavonoids. Often found in the same foods that contain vitamin C.
- Vitamin C. 150g/5½oz of blackcurrants provides more than 100 per cent of the daily recommendation for vitamin C.

blueberries

- Antioxidants and B group vitamins. Antioxidants are essential to eye health.
- Vitamin C.

carambolas (star fruit)

- Great eaten straight, like apples, or sliced into fruit salads, blended into fresh fruit juices, or used as a garnish.
- Top ratings for vitamin C.

cherries

- Beta carotene. Vital for bones and teeth.
- Vitamin C.

dried fruit

- Figs, yellow apricots, Hunza apricots, sultanas, raisins, prunes and dates are great treats for anyone with a sweet tooth. Renowned for their dietary fibre, dried fruits are also packed with beta carotene and potassium. Hunzas (available from most health food shops) are not so well known, but are the tastiest and most nourishing of all apricots. Many dried fruits are treated with sulphite preservatives, which may present a problem for asthmatics.
- Boron. A little-known trace element, needed in small amounts, but essential for healthy bones and teeth. Good for the joints; may be important in helping to prevent osteoporosis and arthritis.
- Magnesium. Works with essential fatty acids, calcium and the B group vitamins to maintain healthy cell production and bones and to support the nervous system and heart.

figs

- One of the 'superfoods'. Fresh figs are delicious in fruit salads. Sweet-tasting, dried figs make great alternatives to sweets and chocolate. They are wonderful chopped into breakfast cereals or eaten as a snack with nuts, seeds and other dried fruit.
- Calcium. Good for the bones.
- Fibre. Packed with dietary fibre, so very valuable for bowel health.
- Magnesium.

grapefruit

- Citrus fruits are a rich source of vitamin C and potassium. Pink and red varieties are high in beta carotene.
- Flavonoids. Often found in the same foods that contain vitamin C. Flavonoids strengthen capillaries, reducing the risk of bleeding and bruising. Deficiency signs are similar to those of vitamin C. Best source: the pith and zest of the fruit.

grapes

- Good source of antioxidants, particularly resveratrol, which scientists believe has anti-cancer and cholesterol-lowering properties.

kiwifruit

- A very fine source of vitamin C – weight for weight, more than twice that of oranges. One kiwifruit provides more than 100 per cent of the daily recommendation for vitamin C.
- Calcium and magnesium. Good for the bones.
- Fibre.
- Small amounts of iron and B group vitamins.

lemons

- Have a reputation as one of the best skin foods; dabbing fresh lemon juice onto the skin, and massaging it in with a little extra virgin olive oil, is an old remedy for improving skin condition and reducing wrinkles.
- Flavonoids.
- Vitamin C.

limes

- An excellent source of vitamin C – 125ml/4fl oz of lime juice provides 30mg, about half the adult daily requirement.

mangoes

- Good source of carotenoids, which are excellent antioxidants.
- Vitamin C.
- Vitamin E.
- Niacin.
- Potassium.

melons

- A rich source of carotenoids, which are excellent antioxidants (particularly cantaloupe or orange-fleshed melons).
- Flavonoids.

nectarines

- Good source of carotenoids, which are excellent antioxidants.
- Vitamin C. Make a super-C juice by blending nectarines with kiwifruit, a squeeze of fresh lemon and honey.

oranges

- One medium-sized orange provides more than the adult daily requirement of vitamin C.
- Folate, thiamine, potassium.

papayas (pawpaws)

- Papayas and pawpaws contain papain, an enzyme that is similar to the digestive juice pepsin, so are good eaten after a meal.
- Flavonoids.
- Good source of carotenoids, which are excellent antioxidants.
- Vitamin C.

peaches

- Good source of carotenoids, which are excellent antioxidants.

pineapples

- Vitamin C. Choose fresh ones where possible; canning can destroy some of the vitamin C content. One of the few fruits (papaya and pawpaw are others) that is best taken directly after a meal, because it contains natural digestive enzymes that help to break down other food. Always swill the mouth and teeth with water after eating pineapple. It can erode tooth enamel very easily.

raspberries

- B group vitamins and antioxidants that are essential for healthy eyes.
- Good source of carotenoids, which are excellent antioxidants.
- Vitamin C.

strawberries

- B group vitamins and antioxidants that are essential for healthy eyes.
- Good source of carotenoids, which are excellent antioxidants.
- Vitamin C.

Vegetables

artichokes

- A natural diuretic and good for the digestion. Contains cyanarin, which is believed to protect the liver.
- Beta carotene, folate, most minerals.

asparagus

- Chock-full of antioxidants, vitamin C, beta carotene and folate. An excellent diuretic that helps rid the body of salt and excess water.
- Beta carotene. Good for the eyes and immune function.
- Chromium. Helps to balance blood glucose and blood fats and to protect the nervous system.
- Vitamin E. Prolongs cell life, hastens wound healing and helps to reduce scarring. Research suggests that vitamin E may be more effective when taken with other antioxidants, especially selenium and vitamins A and C. Easy bruising and dry skin are common signs of deficiency.

bamboo shoots

- Contain trace amounts of vitamin C, calcium and iron.
- Potassium.

beans, green

- Fibre.
- Vitamin C.

beetroot

- Washed and peeled beetroot with a handful of grapes, an apple and a couple of carrots makes a delicious, fruit-flavoured and beautifully coloured red juice.
- Chromium. Helps to balance blood glucose and blood fats, and to protect the nervous system.
- Fabulous for folate, vitamin C, carotenoids and potassium.

brassicas

- The brassicas have important immune-boosting properties. This group includes Brussels sprouts, all kinds of cabbage (including pak choy and red cabbage), Chinese broccoli, green and purple broccoli/calabrese, cauliflower and kale. Brassicas are good bone-boosting foods. The stalks, unless too tough to use, should always be sliced up and included in the dish, as they are a rich source of minerals. Kale and Chinese broccoli are especially high in calcium.
- Vitamin C. Good for the immune system. Some vitamin E, a few B vitamins, folate.
- Sulphoraphane, calcium, magnesium, silica, iron. Sulphoraphane is an important anti-cancer chemical.
- Rich in dietary fibre.

broccoli

- Broccoli stalks are particularly rich in calcium. Tiny raw florets added to salads will raise a meal's vitamin C content.
- Flavonoids.
- High scores for sulphoraphane, beta carotene, folate, potassium, magnesium, calcium.

carrots

- Contain varying amounts of dietary fibre, beta carotene and phenols (sometimes listed as polyphenols) – powerful antioxidant substances which scientists believe may also have immune-boosting properties.
- Rich in carotenoids, which include beta carotene. Five to six servings of these brightly coloured foods each day could reduce significantly the risk of cancer and heart disease, and could mean catching fewer viruses.
- Beta carotene. Vital for bones, teeth, eyes and immune function. Cooking or juicing increases the bio-availability of the carotene. Helps keep eyes healthy and boost the immune system.
- Carrots also contain small amounts of calcium.

celery

- Great in salads and juiced with other vegetables such as carrot and watercress, then sweetened with apple.
- Vitamin C. 300g/11oz of chopped celery provides 10 per cent of the daily recommendation for vitamin C.

dandelion leaves

- Freshly picked young leaves can give a nutritious boost to salads. Naturally diuretic.

garlic

- Modern science has now confirmed that garlic taken regularly reduces cholesterol levels and blood viscosity (stickiness) and boosts immunity. It also has antibacterial properties. Garlic and onions may also block the formation of carcinogenic compounds.
- Garlic and onions may reduce the risk of thrombosis and hypertension.
- Garlic might help in the treatment of nasal congestion.
- Raw garlic is more effective than cooked, and the odour is less strong if garlic is eaten regularly. Those who cannot tolerate garlic (it can cause indigestion in some people) might consider garlic capsules.
- Selenium. A trace element now recognised as a vital antioxidant, being important not only for a strong immune system but also for a healthy heart and circulation, and for the joints.

ginger, fresh root

- When used as a seasoning, fresh ginger contributes trace amounts of minerals.

green vegetables, leafy

- Because of their antioxidant properties, leafy green vegetables are also important foods for healthy eyes, helping to reduce the risk of cataracts and an age-related eye condition known as macular degeneration.
- Boron. A little-known trace element essential for healthy bones and teeth. Good for the joints; may be important in helping to prevent osteoporosis and arthritis. Like selenium, boron levels in food will depend very much on soil status.
- Calcium. For healthy blood, blood vessels, skin, bones and muscle tissue. Calcium combines with vitamin C to help form collagen. Essential for the proper utilisation of essential fatty acids, and also for a healthy nervous system.
- Magnesium. Works with essential fatty acids, calcium and the B group vitamins. Essential for the nervous system and maintaining healthy cell production.
- Selenium. An antioxidant and anti-inflammatory, selenium boosts immune function and improves resistance to infection. Essential for healthy skin, nails and hair.
- The B group vitamins: thiamin (B_1), riboflavin (B_2), niacin (B_3), pantothenic acid (B_5), pyridoxine (B_6), cyanocobalamin (B_{12}), folate, biotin. For the repair and regeneration of skin tissue, to support the nervous system and for deriving energy from food. Deficiency signs include sensitive skin, 'tingling' sensations in the limbs, cracks or sores, especially around the mouth and nose, and itchy, inflamed eyes.
- Vitamin C. Used in the manufacture of collagen, the 'glue' that gives skin its elasticity and support. Vital for wound healing and resistance to infection.
- Vitamin E. Prolongs cell life, hastens wound healing and helps reduce scarring. A vital antioxidant. Research suggests that vitamin E may be more effective when taken with other antioxidants, especially selenium and vitamins A and C.

onions

- Selenium. A trace element now recognised as a vital antioxidant, essential for healthy skin, nails and hair. Flaking or bleeding nails, poor wound healing, dull, dry hair and dry skin can indicate selenium deficiency.

parsley

- A natural diuretic and digestive aid. All culinary herbs are rich in nutrients. Including them in salads and cooking is a good way to add extra vitamins and minerals.
- An abundance of potassium, folate and carotene.
- Beta carotene. Good for the eyes and immune function.
- Iron. Essential for healthy blood. Pale, brittle nails and pale skin may indicate iron deficiency.
- Vitamin C.

peppers (capsicums)

- Rich in vitamin C. Used in the manufacture of collagen, the 'glue' that gives skin its elasticity and support. Vital for wound healing and resistance to infection.

potatoes

- Vitamins B_3 and B_6.
- Vitamin C.

pumpkin

- Beta carotene. Good for the eyes and immune function.

root vegetables

- Fibre.
- Folate and vitamin C.
- Selenium. Has antioxidant and anti-inflammatory properties. Boosts immune function and improves resistance to infection. Essential for healthy skin, nails and hair.

spinach

- Contains antioxidants that are important for healthy eyes. Helps to reduce the risk of cataracts and an age-related eye condition known as macular degeneration.
- Beta carotene. Good for the eyes and immune function.
- Magnesium, carotene and folate. Magnesium is an essential heart nutrient as well as being good for the teeth and bones.

squash

- Excellent source of carotenoids.

sweet potatoes

- Not, in fact, a potato at all but related to the yam family. Red sweet potatoes are loaded with potassium.
- Beta carotene. Good for the eyes and immune function.

tomatoes

- Tomatoes are worth a special mention because they are particularly rich in vitamin C and lycopene; they also contain some dietary fibre. Tomatoes belong to the deadly nightshade family and were once thought to be poisonous. Blamed by some for aggravating arthritis and food allergies, tomatoes have more recently been hailed as an anti-cancer food (mainly for prostate cancers, so they are especially advisable for men). Worth including in the diet several times each week. Lycopene (a carotene) is released when tomatoes are cooked, and better absorbed when eaten with a little oil.
- Selenium.

watercress

- Beta carotene.
- Vitamin C.

Fish

fresh fish

- Magnesium. As important as calcium for maintaining healthy muscles, bones and teeth. An essential heart nutrient.
- Selenium. A vital antioxidant, being important not only for a strong immune system but also for a healthy heart and circulation, and for the joints. Anti-inflammatory; improves resistance to infection; essential for healthy skin, nails and hair.

oily fish

- Oily fish – especially sardines, mackerel, salmon, pilchards, sprats, tuna and trout – are rich in omega-3 essential fatty acids. These are vital for healthy heart function and circulation, and they reduce the stickiness of blood and help to improve the ratio of good cholesterol (high-density lipoprotein – HDL) to bad cholesterol (low-density lipoprotein – LDL). Essential fatty acids are vital for every cell in the body to function properly.

salmon

- Vitamins A and D.
- Vitamins B_1, B_2, B_3, B_5, B_6, B_{12} and biotin.
- Calcium (canned salmon only) and magnesium. Essential for healthy blood, blood vessels, skin, teeth, bones, heart and muscle tissue. Calcium also combines with vitamin C to help form collagen. The all-important essential fatty acids won't be properly utilised without calcium.
- Omega-3 group of essential fatty acids. Important for good sight, among other things.

sardines

- Calcium (canned sardines only) and magnesium. Essential for healthy blood, blood vessels, skin, teeth, bones, heart and muscle tissue. Calcium also combines with vitamin C to help form collagen. The all-important essential fatty acids won't be properly utilised without calcium.
- Omega-3 group of essential fatty acids. Important for good sight, among other things.
- Zinc (canned sardines only). Boosts immune function and essential for maintaining healthy skin.

seafood

- Chromium. Helps to balance blood glucose and blood fats and to protect the nervous system.
- Selenium.
- Zinc. Essential for wound healing and the healthy growth and repair of cells. Excessively oily or very dry skin, persistent infections, white marks on fingernails and slow wound healing are all signs of zinc deficiency.

Meat

lamb

- B group vitamins.
- Iron.
- Magnesium. As important as calcium for maintaining healthy muscles, bones and teeth. An essential heart nutrient.
- Zinc.

lamb's kidney

- Selenium. A vital antioxidant, being important not only for a strong immune system but also for a healthy heart and circulation, and for the joints. Anti-inflammatory; improves resistance to infection; essential for healthy skin, nails and hair.

lamb's liver

- Vitamin A. Liver is one of the highest providers of retinol.
- The B group vitamins: thiamin (B_1), riboflavin (B_2), niacin (B_3), pantothenic acid (B_5), pyridoxine (B_6), cyanocobalamin (B_{12}), folate, biotin. Essential for the repair and regeneration of skin tissue, to support the nervous system and for the release of energy from food. Deficiency signs include sensitive skin, 'tingling' sensations in the limbs, cracks or sores, especially around the mouth and nose, and itchy, inflamed eyes.
- Chromium. Helps to balance blood glucose and blood fats and to protect the nervous system.
- Iron.
- Selenium.
- Zinc.

poultry

- Protein.
- B group vitamins.
- Zinc. Boosts immune function and essential for maintaining healthy skin.

stock (made with bones)

- Calcium. An essential heart nutrient as well as being good for the teeth and bones.

Cereals

millet

- Zinc. Essential for wound healing, healthy growth and repair of cells. Excessively oily or very dry skin, persistent infections, white marks on fingernails and slow wound healing are all signs of zinc deficiency.

oats

- Good source of soluble fibre, which may help reduce cholesterol.
- Vitamin B_1.
- Small amounts of vitamins B_2, B_3, B_6 and folate.
- Zinc. Essential for wound healing, healthy growth and repair of cells. Excessively oily or very dry skin, persistent infections, white marks on fingernails and slow wound healing are all signs of zinc deficiency.

pasta

- Protein.
- Vitamins B_1, B_3.
- Iron.
- Small amounts of magnesium, phosphorus and zinc.

rice (brown)

- Essential fatty acids.
- Magnesium. As important as calcium for maintaining healthy muscles, bones and teeth.
- Selenium.
- Zinc.
- Much more nourishing than white rice, brown rice is also an excellent source of potassium, vitamin B_3, vitamin E and folate – and dietary fibre.

rye

- Zinc. Essential for wound healing and the healthy growth and repair of cells. Excessively oily or very dry skin, persistent infections, white marks on fingernails and slow wound healing are all signs of zinc deficiency.

wholegrains

- The B group vitamins.
- Chromium.
- Magnesium.
- Selenium.
- Vitamin E.

Beans and pulses

- The B group vitamins: thiamin (B_1), riboflavin (B_2), niacin (B_3), pantothenic acid (B_5), pyridoxine (B_6), cyanocobalamin (B_{12}), folate, biotin. Essential for the repair and regeneration of skin tissue, to support the nervous system and for the release of energy from food. Deficiency signs include sensitive skin, 'tingling' sensations in the limbs, cracks or sores around the mouth and nose, and itchy, inflamed eyes.
- Iron. Essential for healthy blood. Pale, brittle nails and pale skin may indicate iron deficiency.
- Magnesium. Magnesium-rich foods, such as pulses, are just as important as calcium for maintaining healthy muscles, bones and teeth. An essential heart nutrient. Works with essential fatty acids, calcium and the B group vitamins to support the nervous system and maintain healthy cell production.
- Vitamin B_2. Deficiency symptoms can include conjunctivitis, bloodshot eyes and cataracts.
- Zinc. Boosts immune function.

chickpeas

- Zinc. Boosts immune function and essential for maintaining healthy skin.

lentils

- Zinc. Boosts immune function and essential for maintaining healthy skin.

peas

- Vitamin C.
- Fibre.
- Folate.
- Small amounts of iron, zinc and magnesium.

red kidney beans

- Zinc. Boosts immune function and essential for maintaining healthy skin.

soya beans

- Calcium. Essential for healthy blood, blood vessels, skin, bones and muscle tissue. The all-important essential fatty acids won't be properly utilised without calcium. Soya beans are thought by some people to help balance hormones.
- Good source of phytoestrogens, which may help reduce the risk of breast and prostate cancer.
- Tofu (bean curd) is an excellent source of protein for vegetarians; rich in calcium, magnesium and iron. Also contains some vitamin E.

Dairy products

butter

- Vitamin A. Good for the eyes. To avoid to much fat in your diet, use in moderation.

buttermilk

- Calcium.

cheese

- Calcium.
- Vitamin A. Good for the eyes.
- Vitamin B_2. Deficiency symptoms can include conjunctivitis, bloodshot eyes and cataracts.
- Zinc. Essential for wound healing and the healthy growth and repair of cells. Excessively oily or very dry skin, persistent infections, white marks on fingernails and slow wound healing are all signs of zinc deficiency.
- Use in moderation and choose low-fat cheeses as much as possible.

eggs

- Protein.
- Chromium. Helps to balance blood glucose and blood fats and to protect the nervous system.
- Selenium and small amounts of iron and zinc.
- Vitamin A. Good for the eyes.
- Vitamin B_2. Deficiency symptoms can include conjunctivitis, bloodshot eyes and cataracts.
- Eggs provide some vitamins B_3, B_{12}, D and E, and folate.

yoghurt

- Calcium.
- Yoghurt with live and active cultures is beneficial not only to the digestion but also to the gut generally, being a valuable source of friendly flora. Topically, live yoghurt can be used to soothe mild sunburn, as a face pack and to treat vaginal and oral thrush.
- Yoghurt provides easily digestible protein, magnesium, potassium, zinc, vitamins B_1 and B_2, and vitamin A.
- Vitamin B_2. Deficiency symptoms can include conjunctivitis, bloodshot eyes and cataracts.

Nuts

- All contain potassium, magnesium, selenium, iron and zinc. They are valuable also for their dietary fibre and their monounsaturated and polyunsaturated fatty acid content. For best nutrient value, nuts should be bought fresh and unbroken, not salted, crushed or roasted.
- The B group vitamins. Vital for the repair and regeneration of skin tissue, to support the nervous system and for the release of energy from food.
- Calcium. For healthy blood, blood vessels, skin, bones and muscle tissue. Calcium combines with vitamin C to help form collagen.
- Iron. Essential for healthy blood. Pale, brittle nails and pale skin may indicate iron deficiency.

- Zinc. Essential for wound healing and the healthy growth and repair of cells. Excessively oily or very dry skin, persistent infections, white marks on fingernails and slow wound healing are all signs of zinc deficiency.

almonds

- Calcium.
- Magnesium.
- Omega-6 essential fatty acids.
- Potassium, selenium, iron and zinc.

Brazil nuts

- Calcium.
- Magnesium.
- Omega-6 essential fatty acids.
- Potassium, selenium, iron and zinc.
- Valuable also for their dietary fibre and their monounsaturated and polyunsaturated fatty acid content.

cashew nuts

- Magnesium.

hazelnuts

- Boron.
- Potassium, magnesium, iron and zinc.
- Valuable also for their dietary fibre and their monounsaturated and polyunsaturated fatty acid content.

macadamia nuts

- Potassium and iron.
- Valuable also for their dietary fibre and their monounsaturated and polyunsaturated fatty acid content.

walnuts

- Omega-3 essential fatty acids.

Seeds

- Edible seeds include pumpkin, sesame, sunflower, poppy, celery, dill, fennel and fenugreek seeds and linseeds. Rich in essential fatty acids. Seeds are providers of zinc, potassium, magnesium and iron. Sunflower seeds are especially rich in vitamin E. Sesame seeds are high in calcium.
- The B group vitamins: thiamin (B_1), riboflavin (B_2), niacin (B_3), pantothenic acid (B_5), pyridoxine (B_6), cyanocobalamin (B_{12}), folate, biotin. Essential for the repair and regeneration of skin tissue, to support the nervous system and for the release of energy from food. Deficiency signs include sensitive skin, 'tingling' sensations in the limbs, cracks or sores, especially around the mouth and nose, and itchy, inflamed eyes.
- Calcium. Essential for healthy blood, blood vessels, skin, bones and muscle tissue. Calcium combines with vitamin C to help form collagen. The all-important essential fatty acids won't be properly utilised without calcium. Apart from leading to weakened bones, too little calcium has a detrimental effect upon the nervous system, resulting in muscle spasm.
- Iron. Essential for healthy blood. Pale, brittle nails and pale skin may indicate iron deficiency.
- Vitamin E. Prolongs cell life, hastens wound healing and helps reduce scarring. A vital antioxidant. Research suggests that vitamin E may be more effective when taken with other antioxidants, especially selenium and vitamins A and C. Easy bruising and dry skin are common signs of deficiency.
- Zinc. Essential for wound healing and the healthy growth and repair of cells.

linseeds and flaxseeds

- Rich in essential fatty acids. Contain zinc, potassium, magnesium and iron.

pumpkin seeds

- Contain essential fatty acids, potassium, magnesium and iron.
- Zinc. Boosts immune function.

sesame seeds

- Calcium. Essential for healthy blood, blood vessels, skin, bones and muscle tissue. Calcium combines with vitamin C to help form collagen. The all-important essential fatty acids won't be properly utilised without calcium.
- Vitamin E. Prolongs cell life, hastens wound healing and helps reduce scarring. A vital antioxidant.
- Rich in essential fatty acids. Contain small amounts of magnesium, phosphorus and iron.
- Tahini, made from sesame seeds, has the same nutrients.

sunflower seeds

- Rich in essential fatty acids. Also high in zinc, potassium, magnesium, vitamins B_3 and B_6, and folate.
- Sunflower seeds are especially rich in vitamin E.

Oils

almond oil

- Omega-6 essential fatty acids.

cold-pressed oils

- Cold-pressed oils include sunflower, sesame, walnut, safflower, soy bean and linseed oil, and extra virgin olive oil. Most mass-produced cooking oils are processed and refined using heat and solvents. Cold pressing is a more expensive method, but retains more of the natural goodness of the oil – in particular, substances known as essential fatty acids, or EFAs. As polyunsaturated oils tend to be less stable when heated, it's best to keep them for salads and light cooking. Extra virgin olive oil is predominantly monounsaturated and more stable at higher temperatures, although frying impairs its flavour. Try to include a tablespoon of some kind of cold-pressed, unrefined oil in your diet every day and keep these oils in the refrigerator so that they retain their freshness.
- Vitamin E. Hastens wound healing and helps reduce scarring.

fish oils

- Rich in omega-3 essential fatty acids, which are found in every cell structure in the body and are vital for good muscle tone, healthy hair, strong nails, hormone production and healthy skin. Weak flaking nails, dry hair and flaking skin are common signs of deficiency.
- Vitamin A-rich foods, such as cod liver oil, are good for eyes, help to protect cell membranes and may reduce the risk of glaucoma.
- Vitamin D.

olive oil (extra virgin)

- Rich in monounsaturates. The best oil for cooking although frying impairs its flavour; also makes excellent salad dressings.

Sugars

blackstrap molasses

- Calcium.
- Iron. Essential for healthy blood. Pale, brittle nails, pale skin and constant lethargy may indicate iron deficiency.
- Magnesium.

honey

- Ordinary honey has about the same nutritional profile as sugar. Health food advocates maintain that best-quality, cold-pressed raw honey is usually single source (not blended), nearly always organic, and usually produced without the need to feed bees on sugar. Like all sugars, honey should be used in moderation.

notes *on* ingredients

Whenever possible, use fresh vegetables, fruit and juices. Organically grown produce is preferable as it is free from chemical fertilisers and pesticides. Cooking vegetables by steaming or microwaving is the best way to retain their nutrients.

Organic dairy products – milk, butter, cheese and yoghurt – are available in health food shops and major supermarkets. For cooking, thick, creamy Greek-style yoghurt has the best consistency. People who are allergic to or intolerant of cow's milk can use goat's milk, and sheep's or goat's milk yoghurt. Although no significant nutritional difference between organic and intensively farmed produce has yet been proved, you may prefer to use free-range lamb, poultry and eggs.

Although only an extremely small percentage of eggs contain salmonella bacteria – which, if the eggs are improperly handled, can multiply and cause salmonellosis – it is worth noting that mayonnaise and dishes that call for uncooked eggs can possibly cause illness. To reduce this risk greatly, buy only very fresh eggs in unbroken shells, refrigerate them immediately, and use them as quickly as possible. Wash your hands and all work surfaces and utensils thoroughly before working with eggs. It is best to avoid uncooked eggs altogether if you will be serving children, elderly people, or those with a compromised immune system, or if you live in an area that has experienced outbreaks of salmonellosis.

When a recipe includes olive oil, the best kind to use is extra virgin olive oil. Because it is produced by pressure, rather than by chemical processing, it is thought that more of the antioxidants are preserved to give better nutritional value and flavour. Oils, such as sunflower, sesame, hazelnut and walnut, should be unrefined and cold-pressed. Most mass-produced cooking oils are processed using heat and solvents. Cold-pressed and unrefined oils are more expensive, but are claimed to retain more of the natural goodness of the oils, in particular the essential fatty acids, or EFAs, and vitamin E.

The use of white sugar should be kept to a minimum. Organic brown sugar, molasses, real maple syrup and cold-pressed honey are alternatives that should be used in moderation.

Wholegrains, such as brown rice, oats, rye, millet, barley and couscous, are excellent sources of fibre and B group vitamins. Breads served with a meal should be of the wholegrain variety. For people with gluten sensitivity, gluten-free flours and pasta, made from potato, rice, buckwheat or legumes, are available.

Soy sauce contains some useful minerals, but these include high levels of sodium. Being careful of your salt intake is important if you have high blood pressure. None of the recipes in this book include more than a tablespoon of soy sauce, but some people may prefer to use the reduced-salt version.

notes *on the* recipes

Both metric and imperial measurements are given in the recipes. Use one set of measurements only throughout a recipe, because metric and imperial measurements are not interchangeable. The preparation and cooking times are approximate.

All spoon measurements refer to British Standard measuring spoons. All spoonfuls are level, unless otherwise stated.

1 teaspoon (tsp) = 5ml
1 tablespoon (tbsp) = 15ml (3 teaspoons)

As the Australian tablespoon is 20ml (4 teaspoons), Australian readers should use 3 teaspoons whenever a tablespoon is specified (New Zealand uses British spoons).

Ovens and grills should be preheated to the temperature specified in the recipe. The cooking times for all the recipes in this book are based on the oven or grill being preheated. If using a fan oven, follow the manufacturer's instructions for adjusting the time and temperature.

Frozen dishes may be defrosted in the microwave, or left in the refrigerator for several hours or overnight. *Do not thaw at room temperature unless instructed.*

Fresh herbs are used in many of the recipes. Fresh herbs give a better flavour, but if dried herbs are used instead of fresh, one tablespoon of finely chopped fresh herbs is equivalent to about one teaspoon of dried herbs. This does not apply to recipes where dried herbs only are listed, such as dried *herbes de provence:* a mixture of rosemary, thyme, sage, parsley and bay leaves.

basic recipes

home-made chicken stock

ingredients

- 1 meaty free-range chicken carcass
- 1 onion or 2 leeks, sliced
- 2 carrots, sliced
- 2 celery sticks, chopped
- 1 bay leaf or 1 fresh bouquet garni
- sea salt
- freshly ground black pepper

makes approx
700ml (1¼ pints)

method

1 Break or chop the chicken carcass into pieces and place in a large saucepan.
2 Add the prepared vegetables and bay leaf or bouquet garni with 1.7 litres (3 pints) cold water.
3 Bring to the boil, reduce the heat, then partially cover the pan and simmer gently for about 2 hours. Skim off and discard any scum and fat.
4 Strain the stock through a sieve, then set aside to cool. When cold, remove and discard all the fat.
5 When required for use, season to taste.

If not required immediately, this stock can be kept in the refrigerator in a covered container for up to 3 days, or frozen for up to 3 months.

home-made vegetable stock

ingredients

- 2 onions, sliced
- 1 large carrot, sliced
- 1 leek, sliced
- 4 sticks celery, chopped
- 1 small turnip or 115g (4oz) swede, diced
- 1 parsnip, sliced
- 1 fresh bouquet garni or 1 bay leaf
- sea salt
- freshly ground black pepper

makes approx
1.3 litres (2¼ pints)

method

1 Put the prepared vegetables and bouquet garni or bay leaf in a large saucepan. Add 1.7 litres (3 pints) cold water.
2 Bring to the boil, reduce the heat, then partially cover the pan and simmer gently for 1–1½ hours. Skim off and discard any scum that rises to the surface.
3 Strain the stock through a sieve.
4 Season to taste.

If not required immediately, this stock can be kept in the refrigerator in a covered container for up to 3 days, or frozen for up to 3 months.

mayonnaise

ingredients

- 2 egg yolks
- 1tsp Dijon mustard
- 1tbsp lemon or lime juice
- ½tsp sugar
- ½tsp sea salt
- freshly ground black pepper
- 150ml (¼ pint) olive oil

makes approx
200ml (7fl oz)

To reduce the risk of salmonella when using uncooked eggs, buy only very fresh eggs in unbroken shells, refrigerate them immediately, and use them as quickly as possible. Wash your hands and all work surfaces and utensils thoroughly before working with eggs. It is best to avoid uncooked eggs altogether if you will be serving children, elderly people, or anyone with a compromised immune system.

method

1 Put the egg yolks, mustard, lemon or lime juice, sugar, salt, black pepper and 1tbsp oil into a small blender or food processor. Blend for 30 seconds.

2 With the blades turning, gradually add the remaining oil, pouring it through the funnel in a slow, continuous stream, until the mayonnaise is thick and smooth.

3 Adjust the seasoning, then use immediately or cover and refrigerate for up to 3 days.

french dressing

ingredients

- 6tbsp olive oil
- 2tbsp white wine or cider vinegar, or lemon juice
- 1–2tsp Dijon mustard
- pinch of sugar
- 1 small clove garlic, crushed
- 1–2tbsp chopped fresh mixed herbs
- sea salt
- freshly ground black pepper

makes approx
150ml (¼ pint)

method

1 Put all the ingredients in a small bowl and whisk together until thoroughly mixed. Alternatively, place all the ingredients in a clean, screw-top jar, seal and shake well until thoroughly mixed.

2 Adjust the seasoning and serve immediately or keep in a screw-top jar in the refrigerator for up to 1 week. Shake thoroughly before serving.

body

In this section, you will find healthy recipes containing the best foods to help boost your immune system, keep your heart and circulatory system healthy, encourage strong teeth and bones and help keep joints flexible. Your immune system needs vitamins A and C, plus the minerals zinc and selenium, in order to function well. Oily fish and lamb's liver are rich in vitamin A; sweet potatoes and carrots are rich in beta carotene, which the body can convert into vitamin A. For zinc and selenium, which are also good for the heart, eat seafood, meat, poultry, split peas, pumpkin seeds, lentils, brown rice, kidneys, garlic, Brazil nuts, raw wheatgerm and other grains. Vitamin C is an overall star when it comes to health. Most fruits and vegetables contain some vitamin C, but rich sources include oranges, grapefruit, kiwifruit, lemons, limes, sweet red peppers (capsicums), kale, tomatoes, broccoli and Brussels sprouts.

FOODS

For a healthy heart and good circulation the body needs magnesium, selenium, calcium, vitamin E, and omega-3 and -6 essential fatty acids. Oily fish is rich in omega-3 essential fats, which reduce the risk of blood clots and lower low-density lipoprotein (LDL) – the type of cholesterol that can lead to heart disease. Walnuts, linseeds, sunflower and pumpkin seeds, and their oils, are rich in both omega-3 and -6 fatty acids and also contain vitamin E, which helps to protect the heart and joints. Avocados, wheatgerm and leafy green vegetables, such as broccoli, are all rich in vitamin E. For calcium and magnesium, which are vital for healthy bones and teeth, make sure that you include low-fat dairy products, wheatgerm, almonds, cashews, Brazil nuts, sesame seeds, dark-green leafy vegetables and tofu in your diet. You will find all these foods included in the delicious recipes that follow.

immunity *foods*

VITAMIN A AND *zinc are essential nutrients for the immune system. Foods that are rich in zinc include seafood, poultry, eggs, green peas and beans, brown rice and most pulses. Significant amounts of beta carotene, which can be converted into vitamin A by the body, are found in dark-green leafy vegetables, carrots, and yellow- or orange-coloured fruits such as apricots. The trace element selenium is also important: good sources are meat, grains, brown rice, seafood, fresh fish, eggs, lamb's liver and kidneys and Brazil nuts. Fresh vegetables and fruits also provide some selenium.*

carrot *and* coriander soup

This tasty carrot soup, served with thick slices of fresh wholemeal bread, is ideal for a warming evening meal or snack. Carrots are high in beta carotene (for vitamin A), which has been linked with lowered rates of cancer and heart disease, and is actually more bioavailable from cooked carrots than from raw.

ingredients

- 1tbsp olive oil
- 2 onions, chopped
- 700g (1lb 9oz) carrots, sliced
- 850ml (1½ pints) vegetable stock (see recipe on page 20)
- sea salt
- freshly ground black pepper
- 2–3tbsp chopped fresh coriander
- fresh coriander sprigs, to garnish

serves *four*
preparation time *15 minutes*
cooking time *30 minutes*

method

1 Heat the oil in a large saucepan. Add the onions and cook gently for 5 minutes until softened.

2 Add the carrots, stock and seasoning. Cover, bring to the boil, then reduce the heat and simmer for 25 minutes, stirring occasionally, until the carrots are tender.

3 Remove the pan from the heat and cool slightly, then purée the soup in a food processor.

4 Return the soup to the rinsed-out saucepan. Stir in the chopped coriander, then reheat gently until piping hot, stirring occasionally.

5 Ladle into warmed soup bowls and garnish with the coriander sprigs.

6 Serve with warm wholemeal bread rolls, oatcakes or crispbread.

variations

- *Add the finely grated rind and juice of 1 orange just before serving.*
- *Add 1–2tsp grated fresh peeled root ginger with the carrots.*

freezing instructions

Allow the soup to cool completely, then transfer to a rigid, freezeproof container. Cover, seal and label. Freeze for up to 3 months.

sweet pepper, tomato *and* basil salad

This quick and easy salad makes a colourful and appetising starter. Peppers (capsicums) and tomatoes contain beta carotene (for vitamin A), vitamin C, fibre and antioxidants. Tomatoes are an excellent source of lycopene, which is thought to play a very important role in immune function.

ingredients

- 2 yellow peppers (capsicums)
- 1 red pepper (capsicum)
- 450g (1lb) plum (Roma) tomatoes
- fresh basil sprigs, to garnish

for the dressing

- 4tbsp olive oil
- 1tbsp balsamic vinegar
- pinch of brown sugar
- 2tbsp chopped fresh basil
- sea salt
- freshly ground black pepper

serves *four*
preparation time *15 minutes, plus 1 hour standing time*

method

1 Core, seed and slice the peppers. Slice the tomatoes. Arrange the peppers and tomatoes on a serving platter.
2 To make the dressing, put the oil, vinegar, sugar, basil and seasoning in a small bowl and whisk together.
3 Drizzle the dressing over the peppers and tomatoes. Cover and leave to stand at room temperature for 1 hour, to allow the flavours to blend thoroughly.
4 Garnish with the basil sprigs.
5 Serve with wholemeal bread.

variation

- *Use chopped fresh mixed herbs or chives instead of basil.*

grilled peppers *with* goat's cheese

A combination of grilled peppers (capsicums) and goat's cheese drizzled with a light herb dressing makes a tasty starter. Peppers are a good source of beta carotene and vitamin C, which boost the immune system.

ingredients

- 2 red peppers (capsicums)
- 2 yellow peppers (capsicums)
- 225g (8oz) goat's cheese, diced or sliced
- 16 black olives

for the dressing

- 4tbsp olive oil
- 1–2tbsp chopped fresh mixed herbs
- sea salt
- freshly ground black pepper

serves *four*
preparation time *15 minutes, plus cooling time*
cooking time *10 minutes*

method

1 Preheat the grill to high.
2 Halve, core and seed the peppers. Place them on a rack in a grill pan and grill for about 10 minutes, turning occasionally, until the skin is blackened and the flesh softened.
3 Put the peppers in a covered dish and allow to cool. Remove and discard the skin.
4 Slice the peppers and arrange on four serving plates. Scatter over the cheese.
5 To make the dressing, whisk the oil, herbs and seasoning in a bowl. Drizzle the oil mixture over the cheese and peppers.
6 Top with the black olives.
7 Serve with wholemeal bread or rolls.

variations

- *Use feta or haloumi cheese instead of goat's cheese.*
- *Use chopped fresh basil instead of mixed herbs.*
- *Use half olive and half walnut oil.*

warm seafood salad *with* fresh herbs

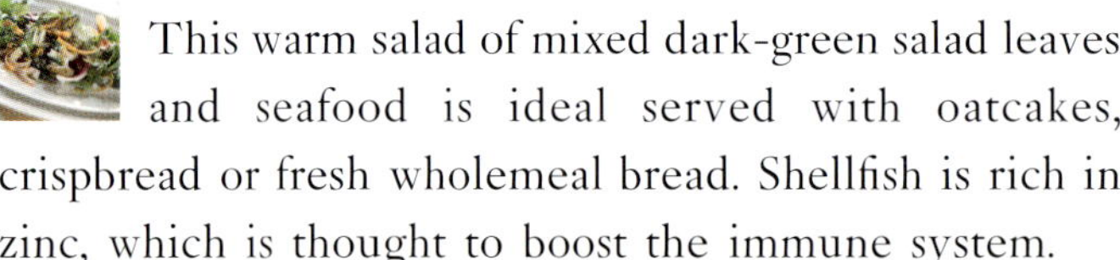

This warm salad of mixed dark-green salad leaves and seafood is ideal served with oatcakes, crispbread or fresh wholemeal bread. Shellfish is rich in zinc, which is thought to boost the immune system.

ingredients

- 2 carrots
- 125g (4½oz) mixed dark-green salad leaves, such as spinach, lollo rosso (coral lettuce), red (ruby) chard, watercress and rocket
- 1tbsp olive oil
- 400g (14oz) packet frozen shelled mixed seafood, defrosted

for the dressing

- 4tbsp olive oil
- 1tbsp unsweetened orange juice
- 2tsp white wine vinegar
- 1tsp Dijon mustard
- 1–2tbsp chopped fresh mixed herbs
- sea salt
- freshly ground black pepper

serves *four*
preparation time *15 minutes*
cooking time *5 minutes*

method

1 Peel the carrots and shave thinly using a potato peeler. Toss the shavings with the salad leaves and arrange on four serving plates.

2 To make the dressing, put the oil, orange juice, vinegar, mustard, herbs and seasoning in a bowl and whisk together. Set aside.

3 Heat the remaining 1tbsp oil in a non-stick wok or large frying pan. Add the seafood and stir-fry for about 5 minutes, until the seafood is cooked.

4 Spoon the cooked seafood over the salad leaves. Give the salad dressing a quick whisk, then drizzle it over the salads.

5 Serve immediately with oatcakes, crispbread or wholemeal bread.

variations

- *Use courgettes (zucchini) instead of carrots.*
- *Use unsweetened apple juice instead of orange juice.*
- *Use wholegrain mustard instead of Dijon mustard.*

peppered salmon *en* papillote

Salmon remains moist and full of flavour when baked in a paper parcel. It is rich in vitamin A, which is important for the immune system.

ingredients

- 2–3tbsp mixed peppercorns
- 4 salmon steaks, each weighing about 175g (6oz)
- juice of 2 limes

serves *four*
preparation time *10 minutes*
cooking time *20–25 minutes*

method

1 Preheat the oven to 180°C/350°F/gas mark 4.

2 Crush the peppercorns coarsely using a pestle and mortar, then sprinkle onto a plate. Press each salmon steak into the pepper, covering both sides completely.

3 Cut four pieces of non-stick baking paper, each large enough to hold one salmon steak in a parcel. Place a salmon steak on each and drizzle over some lime juice. Fold the paper over the fish and twist the edges to secure, making four parcels.

4 Place the parcels on a baking tray and bake for 20–25 minutes, until the flesh just flakes when tested with a fork.

5 Place each unopened parcel on a warmed serving plate and serve with cooked fresh vegetables, such as new potatoes, broccoli florets and carrot sticks.

variations

- *Use tuna steaks instead of salmon.*
- *Use lemon juice instead of lime.*

lemon chicken kebabs *with* herbed rice

These flavoursome kebabs are quick to make and delicious to eat. Chicken and brown rice provide zinc, selenium and B vitamins – good for the immune system and for the healthy growth and repair of cells.

ingredients

- 450g (1lb) skinless, boneless chicken breasts, cut into 2.5cm (1in) cubes
- 2 lemons
- 2tbsp olive oil
- 1 large clove garlic, crushed
- 2tbsp chopped fresh coriander
- sea salt
- freshly ground black pepper
- 225g (8oz) long grain brown rice
- 2 red or yellow peppers (capsicums), seeded and each cut into 8 pieces
- 16 button mushrooms
- 2–3tbsp chopped fresh mixed herbs

serves *four*
preparation time *20 minutes, plus 1 hour marinating time*
cooking time *35 minutes*

method

1 Put the chicken cubes in a shallow, non-metallic dish and set to one side.

2 Finely grate the rind of 1 lemon and squeeze the juice from both lemons. Place the lemon rind and juice in a small bowl with the oil, garlic, coriander and seasoning, and whisk together.

3 Pour the marinade over the chicken and toss to coat completely. Cover and refrigerate for 1 hour.

4 Cook the rice until tender. Keep warm.

5 Meanwhile, preheat the grill to medium. Thread the chicken, peppers and mushrooms onto four long skewers, dividing the ingredients evenly.

6 Place the kebabs on a rack in a grill pan. Grill for about 10 minutes, turning frequently, until the chicken is cooked through and tender. Brush the kebabs regularly with the marinade to prevent them drying out.

7 Stir the herbs and seasoning into the rice, then spoon the rice into a warmed serving dish. Place the kebabs on top.

8 Serve with a shredded mixed vegetable salad.

variations

- *Use turkey breasts instead of chicken breasts.*
- *Use sliced courgettes (zucchini) and cherry tomatoes instead of peppers and mushrooms.*
- *Use the rind and juice of a lime instead of lemons.*

devilled kidneys

The wonderful flavour of kidneys is highlighted in this tasty recipe. Lamb's kidneys are a nutritious food and provide selenium, which is needed by the immune system and helps improve resistance to infection.

ingredients

- 25g (1oz) butter
- 4 shallots (French shallots), thinly sliced
- 12 lamb's kidneys, cored and halved
- 225g (8oz) mushrooms, sliced
- 2tsp English mustard
- dash of Tabasco sauce
- 2tbsp crème fraîche or light sour cream
- sea salt
- freshly ground black pepper
- 2tbsp chopped fresh parsley, to garnish

serves *four*
preparation time *15 minutes*
cooking time *15 minutes*

method

1 Melt the butter in a large non-stick frying pan. Add the shallots and cook gently for 5 minutes, stirring frequently.

2 Add the kidneys and mushrooms, and cook for 5 minutes, stirring occasionally.

3 Stir in the mustard and Tabasco sauce. Cook for a further 3–4 minutes, until the kidneys are cooked, stirring occasionally. Stir in the crème fraîche or sour cream.

4 Season to taste with salt and pepper, and sprinkle with the parsley.

5 Serve on a bed of pasta or rice noodles with a mixed dark-green leaf salad.

variations

- *Add an extra 1tsp mustard for a slightly hotter sauce.*
- *Use lamb's livers, cut into thin strips, instead of kidneys.*
- *Use 1 leek instead of shallots.*

fruit *and* nut coleslaw

This combination of lightly dressed vegetables, fruits and nuts is quick and easy to prepare and makes a great party dish. Whole nuts such as Brazils and almonds are good sources of vitamin E and omega-6 essential fatty acids.

ingredients

- 225g (8oz) green or white cabbage
- 225g (8oz) red cabbage
- 1 large carrot
- 4 sticks celery
- 115g (4oz) raisins
- 115g (4oz) ready-to-eat dried apricots, chopped
- 175g (6oz) mixed Brazil nuts and almonds, roughly chopped

for the dressing

- 8tbsp mayonnaise (see recipe on page 21)
- 4tbsp plain yoghurt
- 3tbsp chopped fresh mixed parsley and chives
- sea salt
- freshly ground black pepper

serves *six*
preparation time *20 minutes, plus 1–2 hours chilling time*

method

1 Shred the cabbage, coarsely grate the carrot, chop the celery and place in a large bowl. Add the dried fruit and nuts, and stir.
2 To make the dressing, mix the mayonnaise, yoghurt, herbs and seasoning together in a small bowl.
3 Spoon the dressing over the cabbage mixture and toss thoroughly. Cover and chill for 1–2 hours before serving.
4 Serve with oven-baked potatoes or slices of crusty wholemeal bread.

variations

- *Use 175g (6oz) sliced mushrooms instead of celery.*
- *Use ready-to-eat dried pears, peaches or mango instead of dried apricots.*
- *Use sultanas instead of raisins.*

green vegetable stir-fry *with* pumpkin seeds

Pumpkin seeds, which are rich in zinc, add flavour and texture to this tasty vegetable stir-fry. Green vegetables provide a wealth of nutrients, including beta carotene (for vitamin A), vitamin C, folate, magnesium and iron.

ingredients

- 225g (8oz) small broccoli florets
- 175g (6oz) green beans, chopped into 2.5cm (1in) lengths
- 2tbsp olive oil
- 1 green pepper (capsicum), seeded and sliced
- 12–16 spring onions, chopped
- 1 clove garlic, crushed
- 115g (4oz) spinach leaves, shredded
- 2tbsp dry sherry
- 1tbsp light soy sauce
- 2–3tbsp pumpkin seeds
- sea salt
- freshly ground black pepper

serves *four*
preparation time *15 minutes*
cooking time *10 minutes*

method

1 Blanch the broccoli florets and green beans in a saucepan of boiling water for 2 minutes, then drain thoroughly.

2 Heat the oil in a non-stick wok or large frying pan. Add the broccoli, beans, pepper, spring onions and garlic, and stir-fry over a high heat for 3–4 minutes.

3 Add the spinach and stir-fry for a further 1–2 minutes.

4 Add the sherry, soy sauce, pumpkin seeds and seasoning, and stir-fry for 1–2 minutes, until the vegetables are cooked.

5 Serve with baked potatoes or on a bed of brown rice.

variations

- *Use sesame oil instead of olive oil.*
- *Use unsweetened apple juice instead of sherry.*

root vegetable *and* lentil stew

This thick, wholesome stew of mixed vegetables and lentils is delicious served with brown rice. Lentils are an excellent source of zinc. Root vegetables provide a range of vitamins and minerals, including vitamin C, folate, potassium and magnesium.

ingredients

- 1tbsp olive oil
- 1 onion, sliced
- 1 clove garlic, crushed
- 2tbsp plain wholemeal or potato flour
- 850ml (1½ pints) vegetable stock (see recipe on page 20)
- 225g (8oz) potatoes, diced
- 225g (8oz) carrots, thinly sliced
- 175g (6oz) swede, diced
- 175g (6oz) parsnips, diced
- 3 sticks celery, chopped
- 225g (8oz) whole green or brown lentils
- 400g (14oz) can tomatoes, chopped
- 2tsp dried mixed herbs
- 1tsp ground cumin
- sea salt
- freshly ground black pepper
- fresh herb sprigs, to garnish

serves *six*
preparation time *15 minutes*
cooking time *55–70 minutes*

method

1 Heat the oil in a large saucepan. Add the onion and garlic, and cook for 3 minutes, stirring.
2 Add the flour and cook for 30 seconds, stirring.
3 Remove the pan from the heat, then gradually add the stock, stirring continuously.
4 Add all the remaining ingredients, except the herb garnish, and stir.
5 Bring gently to the boil, stirring continuously. Cover and simmer for 45–60 minutes, until the vegetables and lentils are cooked and tender, stirring occasionally.
6 Adjust the seasoning.
7 Serve on a bed of brown rice or with mashed potatoes, garnished with the herb sprigs.

variations

- *To cook this dish in the oven, parboil sliced potatoes, then drain thoroughly and toss in a little olive oil. Bring the stew to the boil, as directed, then transfer to an ovenproof casserole dish. Arrange the potatoes over the top, covering the vegetable mixture completely. Bake in a preheated oven at 200°C/400°F/gas mark 6 for about 1 hour, until cooked.*
- *Use sweet potatoes and turnips instead of potatoes and swede. You could also add a few chopped kale or other cabbage leaves for added vitamin C.*

freezing instructions

Allow to cool completely, then transfer to a rigid, freezeproof container. Cover, seal and label. Freeze for up to 3 months. Defrost, and reheat gently in a saucepan until piping hot.

fig *and* apple oat crunchies

These oat crunchies make a tasty sweet treat, ideal for a packed lunch or a light snack. Figs, both fresh and dried, are packed with dietary fibre, iron, magnesium and calcium.

ingredients

- 115g (4oz) butter
- 115g (4oz) light brown sugar
- 2tbsp honey
- 175g (6oz) rolled oats
- 1tsp ground mixed spice
- 85g (3oz) ready-to-eat dried figs, finely chopped
- 25g (1oz) ready-to-eat dried apples, finely chopped

makes *eight to ten*
preparation time *15 minutes*
cooking time *20–30 minutes*

method

1 Preheat the oven to 180°C/350°F/gas mark 4.
2 Lightly grease a shallow 18cm (7in) square cake tin.
3 Put the butter, sugar and honey in a saucepan and heat gently until melted. Remove from the heat.
4 Stir in the oats, mixed spice, figs and apples, and mix well. Transfer the mixture to the prepared tin and press it down well.
5 Bake for 20–30 minutes, until golden brown.
6 Mark into fingers or squares while still warm, then allow to cool completely in the tin. Break into fingers or squares to serve.

variations

- *Use maple syrup instead of honey.*
- *Use muesli, or a mixture of oats and barley or rye flakes.*

freezing instructions

Allow to cool completely, then wrap in foil or seal in freezer bags and label. Freeze for up to 3 months. Defrost thoroughly for several hours at room temperature before serving.

red fruit jellies

These delicious fruit jellies are a summertime treat for all the family. Red fruits contain beta carotene (for vitamin A) and vitamin C, as well as antioxidants which may help to boost the immune system.

ingredients

- 425ml (¾ pint) unsweetened apple juice
- 115g (4oz) sugar
- juice of 1 lemon
- 11g (¼oz) sachet powdered gelatine
- 150ml (¼ pint) red wine
- 225g (8oz) mixed prepared red fruits, such as small strawberries, raspberries and loganberries
- fresh mint sprigs, to decorate

serves *six*
preparation time *15 minutes, plus setting time*
cooking time *10 minutes*

method

1 Put the apple juice and sugar in a saucepan and heat gently, stirring occasionally until the sugar has dissolved. Bring to the boil, then simmer for 5 minutes.
2 Put the lemon juice in a bowl with 2tbsp water and sprinkle the gelatine on top. Leave to soak for a couple of minutes, then place the bowl over a pan of simmering water and stir until dissolved.
3 Stir the liquid gelatine and the red wine into the sugar syrup and mix well. Set aside to cool slightly.
4 Arrange the fruits in serving glasses. Pour over a little of the jelly mixture. Cool slightly, then chill until set.
5 Pour over the remaining liquid jelly. Chill until set.
6 Decorate with the mint sprigs and serve with a dollop of plain yoghurt,crème fraîche or light sour cream.

variations

- *Use white or rosé wine.*
- *Use unsweetened grape juice instead of apple juice.*

chocolate-dipped fruit *and* nut platter

This mouthwatering array of chocolate-dipped fruits and whole nuts is hard to resist for a special treat. All fresh fruits contain nutrients that are essential to a well-functioning immune system.

ingredients

- 450g (1lb) fresh firm fruit, such as kiwifruit, pineapple, apricots, peaches and strawberries
- 225g (8oz) plain (dark) chocolate, broken into squares
- 225g (8oz) whole shelled mixed nuts, such as Brazil nuts, almonds, pecan nuts and cashew nuts

serves *six*
preparation time *30 minutes*

method

1 Line two baking trays with non-stick baking paper and set to one side.

2 Peel the kiwifruit and pineapple. Stone the apricots and peaches. Cut the fruit into slices or wedges, but leave the strawberries whole.

3 Put the chocolate in a small bowl over a pan of hot (but not boiling) water, ensuring that the bottom of the bowl does not touch the water. Stir until the chocolate has melted, then remove the pan from the heat.

4 Make sure the surface of the fruit is dry. Holding one end of a piece of fruit in your fingers, or with a fork, half dip it in the melted chocolate. Lift out and hold over the bowl for a few seconds to drain. Carefully place the dipped fruit onto a prepared baking tray.

5 Repeat with the remaining fruit and the nuts until all the ingredients are used up. Leave to dry completely before removing from the paper.

6 Arrange on a serving platter and serve immediately.

variations

- *Dip ready-to-eat dried fruits, such as whole apricots, large raisins, dates or bananas, into melted chocolate.*
- *Dip pieces of crystallised fruit into melted chocolate.*

an apple *a* day...

HELP KEEP THE *doctor away and stay optimally nourished with this delicious and nutritious immune-boosting menu suggestion from the immunity foods section. The vitamins and minerals in these recipes will help your immune system defend against attacks by viruses and bacteria.*

carrot *and* coriander soup

A starter rich in beta carotene (for vitamin A), which may help to reduce the risk of cancer and heart disease.

ingredients

- 1tbsp olive oil
- 2 onions, chopped
- 700g (1lb 9oz) carrots, sliced
- 850ml (1½ pints) vegetable stock (see recipe on page 20)
- sea salt
- freshly ground black pepper
- 2–3tbsp chopped fresh coriander
- fresh coriander sprigs, to garnish

serves *four*
preparation time *15 minutes*
cooking time *30 minutes*

method

1 Heat the oil in a large saucepan. Add the onions and cook gently for 5 minutes until softened.
2 Add the carrots, stock and seasoning. Cover, bring to the boil, then reduce the heat and simmer for 25 minutes, stirring occasionally, until the carrots are tender.
3 Remove the pan from the heat and cool slightly, then purée the soup in a food processor.
4 Return the soup to the rinsed-out saucepan. Stir in the chopped coriander, then reheat gently until piping hot, stirring occasionally.
5 Ladle into warmed soup bowls and garnish with the coriander sprigs.
6 Serve with warm wholemeal bread rolls, oatcakes or crispbread.

lemon chicken kebabs *with* herbed rice

Chicken and brown rice are a valuable source of zinc, selenium and B vitamins – vital to the immune system and important for the healthy growth and repair of cells.

ingredients

- 450g (1lb) skinless, boneless chicken breasts, cut into 2.5cm (1in) cubes
- 2 lemons
- 2tbsp olive oil
- 1 large clove garlic, crushed
- 2tbsp chopped fresh coriander
- sea salt
- freshly ground black pepper
- 225g (8oz) long grain brown rice
- 2 red or yellow peppers (capsicums), seeded and each cut into 8 pieces
- 16 button mushrooms
- 2–3tbsp chopped fresh mixed herbs

serves *four*
preparation time *20 minutes, plus 1 hour marinating time*
cooking time *35 minutes*

method

1 Put the chicken cubes in a shallow, non-metallic dish and set to one side.

2 Finely grate the rind of 1 lemon and squeeze the juice from both lemons. Place the lemon rind and juice in a small bowl with the oil, garlic, coriander and seasoning, and whisk together.

3 Pour the marinade over the chicken and toss to coat completely. Cover and refrigerate for 1 hour.

4 Cook the rice until tender. Keep warm.

5 Meanwhile, preheat the grill to medium. Thread the chicken, peppers and mushrooms onto four long skewers, dividing the ingredients evenly.

6 Place the kebabs on a rack in a grill pan. Grill for about 10 minutes, turning frequently, until the chicken is cooked through and tender. Brush the kebabs regularly with the marinade to prevent them drying out.

7 Stir the herbs and seasoning into the rice, then spoon the rice into a warmed serving dish. Place the kebabs on top.

8 Serve with a shredded mixed vegetable salad.

red fruit jellies

All fresh fruits are vital to boost resistance to infection.

ingredients

- 425ml (¾ pint) unsweetened apple juice
- 115g (4oz) sugar
- juice of 1 lemon
- 11g (¼oz) sachet powdered gelatine
- 150ml (¼ pint) red wine
- 225g (8oz) mixed prepared red fruits, such as small strawberries, raspberries and loganberries
- fresh mint sprigs, to decorate

serves *six*
preparation time *15 minutes, plus setting time*
cooking time *10 minutes*

method

1 Put the apple juice and sugar in a saucepan and heat gently, stirring occasionally until the sugar has dissolved. Bring to the boil, then simmer for 5 minutes.

2 Put the lemon juice in a bowl with 2tbsp water and sprinkle the gelatine on top. Leave to soak for a couple of minutes, then place the bowl over a pan of simmering water and stir until dissolved.

3 Stir the liquid gelatine and the red wine into the sugar syrup and mix well. Set aside to cool slightly.

4 Arrange the fruits in serving glasses. Pour over a little of the jelly mixture. Cool slightly, then chill until set.

5 Pour over the remaining liquid jelly. Chill until set.

6 Decorate with the mint sprigs and serve with plain yoghurt, crème fraîche or light sour cream.

heart *and* circulation foods

*O*MEGA-3 FATTY *acids are vital to healthy heart function because they inhibit blood clotting, control cholesterol and reduce the risk of thrombosis. Oily fish are the main source, but walnuts and seeds also contain significant amounts.*

Vitamin C maintains healthy blood vessels and protects vitamin E (a leading antioxidant, which can help protect against heart disease) from free-radical damage. Vitamin E-rich foods include wholegrains, nuts and oils. Calcium, magnesium and selenium are also vital for a healthy heart.

asparagus *and* broccoli scramble

Green vegetables, such as broccoli and asparagus, are excellent sources of fibre and vitamin C.

ingredients

- 85g (3oz) small broccoli florets
- 85g (3oz) asparagus, cut into 2.5cm (1in) lengths
- 25g (1oz) butter
- 1 leek, washed and thinly sliced
- 8 medium eggs
- 4tbsp milk
- 2tbsp chopped fresh mixed herbs
- sea salt
- freshly ground black pepper
- 25g (1oz) fresh Parmesan cheese, finely grated
- 1tbsp sesame seeds (optional)
- fresh herb sprigs, to garnish

serves *four*
preparation time *10 minutes*
cooking time *15 minutes*

method

1 Cook the broccoli and asparagus in a saucepan of boiling water for about 4 minutes, until tender. Drain and keep warm.

2 Melt the butter in a saucepan, add the leeks and cook for about 10 minutes, stirring occasionally, until softened.

3 Break the eggs into a bowl and lightly beat them with the milk, chopped herbs and seasoning. Pour the egg mixture into the pan and cook gently, stirring, until the mixture begins to thicken.

4 Remove the pan from the heat and continue stirring until the mixture becomes creamy.

5 Stir in the broccoli, asparagus and Parmesan cheese.

6 Serve sprinkled with sesame seeds, if using. Garnish with the herb sprigs.

7 Serve with wholemeal bread or toast.

variations

- *Use sunflower or celery seeds instead of sesame seeds.*
- *Use sliced courgettes (zucchini) instead of asparagus.*
- *Use Cheddar cheese instead of Parmesan cheese.*

brussels sprouts *and* leek soup

This low-fat, tasty and filling soup is ideal for a heart-healthy diet on chilly winter days. Brussels sprouts are also a good source of vitamin C.

ingredients

- 1tbsp olive oil
- 6 shallots (French shallots), chopped
- 225g (8oz) leeks, washed and thinly sliced
- 350g (12oz) potatoes, diced
- 280g (10oz) small Brussels sprouts, quartered
- 850ml (1½ pints) vegetable stock (see recipe on page 20)
- sea salt
- freshly ground black pepper
- 2tbsp chopped fresh parsley
- flatleaf parsley sprigs, to garnish

serves *four*
preparation time *15 minutes*
cooking time *25–30 minutes*

method

1 Heat the oil in a large saucepan. Cook the shallots for 3 minutes.
2 Add the leeks, potatoes and Brussels sprouts. Cook for 5 minutes, stirring occasionally.
3 Stir in the stock and seasoning. Bring to the boil, reduce the heat and simmer for 15–20 minutes, until the vegetables are tender.
4 Cool slightly, then purée in a food processor. Return the soup to the saucepan and reheat.
5 Stir in the chopped parsley and garnish with the parsley sprigs.
6 Serve with wholemeal bread.

variations

- *For a spicy variation, add 2–3tsp curry paste with the stock.*
- *Use sweet potatoes instead of potatoes.*

freezing instructions

Allow to cool completely, then transfer to a rigid, freezeproof container. Cover, seal and label. Freeze for up to 3 months. Defrost, and reheat gently.

crab-stuffed avocado

Lightly dressed crab piled into fresh avocado halves makes a delicious starter. Crab contains selenium, a major antioxidant. Although avocados are high in fat, most of it is of the monounsaturated variety, which helps to keep cholesterol counts down.

ingredients

- 225g (8oz) white crabmeat, flaked
- 3 spring onions, finely chopped
- 1tbsp chopped fresh mixed herbs
- 4tbsp mayonnaise (see recipe on page 21)
- 3tbsp plain yoghurt
- sea salt
- freshly ground black pepper
- 2 ripe avocados
- lemon juice, for brushing
- paprika and lemon wedges, to garnish

serves *four*
preparation time *15 minutes*

method

1 Put the crabmeat, spring onions and herbs in a bowl and mix.
2 In a separate bowl, mix together the mayonnaise and yoghurt, then add to the crab mixture and stir. Season to taste with salt and pepper.
3 Halve the avocados lengthways and remove the stones. Place each half on a serving plate and brush the cut surfaces with a little lemon juice to prevent discoloration.
4 Pile the crab mixture into the avocado halves. Garnish with a sprinkling of paprika and the lemon wedges, and serve with fingers of lightly buttered wholemeal bread or toast.

variations

- *Use canned tuna or salmon or cooked prawns instead of crabmeat.*
- *If fresh crabmeat is not available, use two 170g (6oz) cans white crabmeat in brine, drained and flaked.*

thai-spiced tiger prawns *with* tomato salsa

These Thai-spiced prawns served with a delicious tomato salsa will be popular with anyone who enjoys seafood. Shellfish are a good source of selenium, which helps to keep the heart healthy.

ingredients

for the salsa

- 450g (1lb) tomatoes, skinned, seeded and finely chopped
- 4 sun-dried tomatoes, soaked in warm water, drained and finely chopped
- 2 shallots (French shallots), finely chopped
- 1 clove garlic, crushed
- 1tbsp olive oil
- 1–2tbsp chopped fresh basil
- sea salt
- freshly ground black pepper

for the prawn kebabs

- 2tbsp olive oil
- 2–3tsp Thai 7-spice powder
- 40 raw tiger (or king) prawns, shelled

serves *four*
preparation time *15 minutes, plus 1 hour standing time*
cooking time *4–6 minutes*

method

1 To make the salsa, put the fresh and dried tomatoes, shallots, garlic, olive oil, basil and seasoning in a bowl and mix well. Cover and leave to stand at room temperature for about 1 hour.

2 Preheat the grill to high. Put the remaining 2tbsp oil and the Thai spice powder in a bowl, add the prawns and toss. Thread the prawns onto four skewers.

3 Place the kebabs on a rack in a grill pan. Grill for 2–3 minutes on each side, turning occasionally. The prawns will turn pink when they are cooked.

4 Serve the kebabs with the tomato salsa spooned alongside and a crisp green salad.

variations

- *Use fresh shelled scallops instead of tiger prawns.*
- *Use 4 spring onions instead of the shallots.*
- *Use chopped fresh coriander or flatleaf parsley instead of basil.*

grilled fish steaks *with* fresh lime *and* herbs

Fresh fish steaks, marinated and served with a selection of seasonal fresh vegetables, make a flavourful dish. Fresh fish is rich in magnesium and contains omega-3 fatty acids, important for a healthy heart and good circulation.

ingredients

- 2tbsp olive oil
- finely grated rind and juice of 2 limes
- 2tbsp chopped fresh parsley
- 1tbsp chopped fresh oregano
- sea salt
- freshly ground black pepper
- 4 steaks of firm white fish, such as haddock or gemfish, each weighing about 175g (6oz)
- fresh herb sprigs, to garnish

serves *four*
preparation time *10 minutes, plus 1 hour marinating time*
cooking time *10 minutes*

method

1 Put the oil, lime rind and juice, parsley, oregano and seasoning in a small bowl and whisk until well mixed. Pour into a shallow, non-metallic dish.

2 Add the fish and turn to coat it in the marinade. Cover and refrigerate for about 1 hour.

3 Line a grill rack with foil and preheat the grill to medium. . Place the fish on the rack in a grill pan. Grill for about 5 minutes on each side, until the flesh just flakes when tested with a fork. Brush with the marinade frequently during cooking to prevent the fish from drying out.

4 Garnish with the herb sprigs and serve with cooked fresh vegetables, such as potatoes, broccoli florets and swede or parsnip purée.

variations

- *Use chopped fresh marjoram or basil instead of oregano.*
- *Use lemons instead of limes.*

sweet *and* sour turkey meatballs

These turkey meatballs, cooked in a tasty sauce and served with mashed potatoes and fresh vegetables, are sure to become a family favourite. As well as adding delicious flavour, garlic is thought to help reduce the risk of heart disease by decreasing cholesterol levels and lowering blood pressure.

ingredients

for the meatballs

- 450g (1lb) lean turkey mince
- 4 shallots (French shallots), finely chopped
- 1 clove garlic, crushed
- 115g (4oz) mushrooms, finely chopped
- 2tsp dried *herbes de provence*
- finely grated rind of 1 lemon
- 55g (2oz) fresh wholemeal breadcrumbs
- 2tbsp sun-dried tomato purée (paste)
- sea salt
- freshly ground black pepper
- a little plain wholemeal flour, for dusting
- 1tbsp olive oil

for the sweet and sour sauce

- 1tbsp cornflour
- 4tbsp red wine
- 400g (14oz) can chopped tomatoes, puréed
- 150ml (¼ pint) unsweetened apple juice
- 2tbsp red wine vinegar
- 2tbsp brown sugar
- 1tbsp sun-dried tomato purée (paste)
- fresh herb sprigs, to garnish

serves *four to six*
preparation time *25 minutes, plus 20 minutes chilling time*
cooking time *45 minutes*

method

1 To make the meatballs, put all the meatball ingredients, except the flour and oil, in a bowl and mix well.

2 Roll the mixture into 28 small balls. Sprinkle the flour onto a plate and roll each meatball lightly in the flour. Place the balls on a plate and chill for 20 minutes.

3 Meanwhile, make the sweet and sour sauce. Blend the cornflour with the red wine, then put in a saucepan with all the remaining sauce ingredients and stir to mix. Bring to the boil, stirring continuously, then reduce the heat and simmer gently while cooking the meatballs.

4 Preheat the oven to 180°C/350°F/gas mark 4.

5 Heat the oil in a frying pan and fry the meatballs over a medium heat for 5–10 minutes, turning them frequently, until lightly browned all over. Transfer to a large, shallow, ovenproof dish.

6 Pour the sauce over the meatballs, cover and bake for about 45 minutes, until the meatballs are cooked.

7 Garnish with the herb sprigs and serve with mashed potatoes and cooked spring greens and baby (Dutch) carrots.

variations

- *Use lean chicken or lamb mince instead of turkey.*
- *Use 1 small onion instead of the shallots.*
- *Use courgettes (zucchini) instead of mushrooms.*

chicken *and* mixed pepper stir-fry

For those in a hurry, this stir-fry is quick and easy to make and is good served with noodles or rice. Peppers are super-high in vitamin C.

ingredients

- 1tbsp olive oil
- 1 large clove garlic, finely chopped
- 2.5cm (1in) piece of fresh root ginger, peeled and finely chopped
- 350g (12oz) skinless, boneless chicken breast, cut into strips
- 1 red pepper (capsicum), seeded and sliced
- 1 yellow pepper (capsicum), seeded and sliced
- 1 green pepper (capsicum), seeded and sliced
- 1 courgette (zucchini), thinly sliced diagonally
- 1 leek, washed and thinly sliced
- 115g (4oz) mangetout (snowpeas)
- 2–3tsp cajun seasoning or Chinese 5-spice powder
- 2tbsp dry sherry
- 1tbsp light soy sauce
- sea salt
- freshly ground black pepper
- sesame seeds, to garnish

serves *four*
preparation time *20 minutes*
cooking time *8–10 minutes*

method

1 Heat the oil in a non-stick wok or large frying pan. Add the garlic and ginger, and stir-fry over a high heat for 30 seconds.

2 Add the chicken and stir-fry for 1–2 minutes, until coloured all over. Add the peppers, courgettes, leeks and mangetout, and stir-fry for a further 2–3 minutes.

3 Add the cajun seasoning or 5-spice powder, sherry, soy sauce, salt and pepper, and stir-fry for another 3–4 minutes, until the chicken and vegetables are cooked and tender.

4 Sprinkle with the sesame seeds and serve with rice noodles.

variations

- *Use turkey breast instead of chicken breast.*
- *Use sliced mushrooms instead of mangetout (snowpeas).*
- *Use unsweetened apple juice instead of sherry.*

pasta primavera

Freshly cooked pasta topped with a tasty and nutritious vegetable sauce makes a filling lunch or evening meal. Pasta with mixed vegetables is an excellent source of antioxidants and fibre.

ingredients

- 2 carrots, diced
- 2 courgettes (zucchini), sliced
- 225g (8oz) small broccoli florets
- 115g (4oz) asparagus, cut into 2.5cm (1in) lengths
- 175g (6oz) frozen peas
- 6–8 spring onions, chopped
- 1 clove garlic, crushed
- 400g (14oz) can tomatoes, chopped
- 150ml (¼ pint) vegetable stock (see recipe on page 20)
- sea salt
- freshly ground black pepper
- 1tbsp chopped fresh parsley
- 1tbsp chopped fresh basil
- 350g (12oz) pasta twists (spirals)
- finely grated fresh Parmesan cheese, to serve

serves *four*
preparation time *15 minutes*
cooking time *25 minutes*

method

1 Put the carrots, courgettes, broccoli, asparagus, peas, spring onions, garlic, tomatoes, stock and seasoning in a saucepan and bring to the boil, stirring occasionally.

2 Reduce the heat, cover and simmer for 10 minutes, stirring occasionally. Uncover, increase the heat slightly and cook for a further 5–10 minutes, until the vegetables are cooked and tender, stirring occasionally. Stir the herbs into the vegetable mixture.

3 Meanwhile, cook the pasta until *al dente*. Drain thoroughly.

4 Spoon the pasta onto four warmed serving plates, and spoon the vegetable sauce on top. Serve sprinkled with the Parmesan cheese.

5 Serve with crusty wholemeal bread or rolls.

variations

- *Use mushrooms instead of asparagus.*
- *Use 175g (6oz) diced swede or turnip instead of carrots.*

freezing instructions

The sauce is suitable for freezing. Allow to cool completely, then transfer to a rigid, freezeproof container. Cover, seal and label. Freeze for up to 3 months. Defrost, and reheat gently in a saucepan until piping hot. Serve with freshly cooked pasta.

spicy root vegetables

Root vegetables cooked with spices are a great accompaniment to grilled fish or lean meat. Sweet potatoes are an excellent source of beta carotene, an important antioxidant.

ingredients

- 1 kg (2lb 4oz) mixed root vegetables, such as potatoes, sweet potatoes, parsnips, swede and celeriac, diced
- 3tbsp olive oil
- 1 large clove garlic, crushed
- 1tsp each hot chilli powder, ground cumin and ground coriander
- 2tbsp sunflower or pumpkin seeds (optional)
- sea salt
- freshly ground black pepper
- 2tbsp chopped fresh coriander

serves *four*
preparation time *15 minutes*
cooking time *15–20 minutes*

method

1 Parboil the root vegetables in a large saucepan of boiling water for 5–7 minutes. Drain well.

2 Heat the oil in a large non-stick frying pan. Add the garlic and ground spices, and cook for 30 seconds, stirring.

3 Add the vegetables, toss in the oil and spice mixture, then cook over a medium heat for 10–15 minutes, stirring frequently, until the vegetables are cooked, tender and lightly browned.

4 Add the sunflower or pumpkin seeds, if using, and cook for 1–2 minutes. Season to taste with salt and pepper, and stir in the coriander.

5 Serve with grilled fish or lean meat and cooked fresh vegetables, such as cabbage and green beans.

variations

- *Use sesame seeds instead of sunflower or pumpkin seeds.*
- *Use chopped fresh parsley instead of coriander.*

onion *and* pepper pizza

This home-made pizza, piled high with a mixed pepper and onion topping, makes an appetising snack. Onions are a good source of organic sulphur compounds, which have been linked with lowering cholesterol and blood pressure.

ingredients

for the pizza topping

- 1tbsp olive oil
- 2 onions, sliced
- 2 red peppers (capsicums), seeded and sliced
- 175g (6oz) mushrooms, sliced
- 225g (8oz) can tomatoes, chopped and drained
- 2tbsp tomato purée (paste)
- 2tbsp chopped fresh mixed herbs
- sea salt
- freshly ground black pepper
- 140g (5oz) Cheddar cheese, grated

for the pizza base

- 225g (8oz) plain wholemeal flour
- pinch of salt
- 2tsp baking powder
- 55g (2oz) butter, chopped
- about 100ml (3½fl oz) milk

serves *four to six*
preparation time *25 minutes*
cooking time *25–30 minutes*

method

1 Preheat the oven to 220°C/425°F/gas mark 7. Line a baking tray with non-stick paper.

2 Heat the oil in a saucepan. Add the onions, peppers and mushrooms, cover and cook gently for 10 minutes. Drain.

3 For the base, put the flour, salt and baking powder in a bowl and rub in the butter until the mixture resembles breadcrumbs. Add enough milk to make a soft dough.

4 Roll the dough out on a lightly floured surface, to a circle 25cm (10in) in diameter. Place on the baking tray.

5 Mix the tomatoes and tomato purée together and spread over the base. Sprinkle over the herbs and seasoning.

6 Top with the onion mixture and sprinkle over the cheese.

7 Bake for 25–30 minutes.

8 Serve hot or cold, in slices.

variations

- *Use 8 shallots (French shallots) instead of onions.*
- *Use sliced courgette (zucchini) instead of mushrooms.*

baked bananas *with* cinnamon

This delicious dessert of baked bananas is especially good served with a dollop of crème fraîche, light sour cream or plain yoghurt. Bananas are rich in potassium, which is important for the maintenance of proper blood pressure.

ingredients

- 4tbsp unsweetened orange juice
- 4tbsp honey
- 2tbsp rum
- 4 firm, ripe bananas
- 2 cinnamon sticks, broken in half

serves *four*
preparation time *10 minutes*
cooking time *30 minutes*

method

1 Preheat the oven to 180°C/350°F/gas mark 4.

2 Put the orange juice, honey and rum in a small bowl and mix well.

3 Peel the bananas and slice each in half lengthways. Place in a shallow, ovenproof dish and add the cinnamon sticks.

4 Pour over the orange juice mixture and turn the bananas over to coat.

5 Cover the dish with foil and bake for about 30 minutes, until the bananas are softened.

6 Remove and discard the cinnamon sticks. Serve the bananas on warmed serving plates with the sauce spooned over.

7 Add a dollop of crème fraîche, light sour cream or plain yoghurt, or a scoop of home-made yoghurt ice.

variations

- *For spicy baked bananas, omit the cinnamon and add 2tsp ground mixed spice to the orange juice mixture before baking.*
- *Use fresh peaches or nectarines instead of bananas.*
- *Use maple syrup instead of honey.*
- *Use brandy instead of rum.*
- *To add selenium and essential fatty acids, sprinkle raw wheatgerm and linseeds over the top.*

fruit kebabs *with* lemon sauce

Fresh fruit kebabs served with a tangy lemon sauce make a refreshing light dessert. Kiwifruit and strawberries are good sources of vitamin C, which promotes iron absorption and maintains healthy blood vessels.

ingredients

- 450g (1lb) small strawberries
- 6 kiwifruit, peeled and each cut into 8 pieces

for the lemon sauce

- 2tsp arrowroot
- 3tbsp water
- finely grated rind and juice of 2 lemons
- 4tbsp honey
- fresh mint sprigs, to decorate

serves *four*
preparation time *10 minutes*
cooking time *10 minutes*

method

1 Thread the strawberries and kiwi fruit onto four long or eight short skewers, dividing the fruit evenly between the skewers. Place on four serving plates.

2 Blend the arrowroot with the water and put into a saucepan with the lemon rind and juice, and the honey.

3 Bring slowly to the boil, stirring, until the mixture thickens.

4 Serve the lemon sauce drizzled over or alongside the fruit kebabs. Decorate with mint sprigs.

5 Serve with home-made fruit yoghurt ice for a special treat.

variations

- *The lemon sauce can be served hot or cold.*
- *Replace the strawberries and kiwifruit with other fresh fruit, such as papaya, grapes, mango, pineapple, nectarines and eating apples.*
- *Use lime juice instead of lemon.*

the hungry heart

CONTROL CHOLESTEROL LEVELS, and help to keep your heart and circulation functioning smoothly with this stimulating selection of recipes from the heart and circulation section, rich in vitamin E, omega-3 fatty acids, vitamin C and potassium – all vital for a healthy heart and good circulation.

crab-stuffed avocado

Avocado is rich in vitamin E and crab contains selenium – both essential antioxidants which could help to protect against heart disease.

ingredients

- 225g (8oz) white crabmeat, flaked
- 3 spring onions, finely chopped
- 1tbsp chopped fresh mixed herbs
- 4tbsp mayonnaise (see recipe on page 21)
- 3tbsp plain yoghurt
- sea salt
- freshly ground black pepper
- 2 ripe avocados
- lemon juice, for brushing
- paprika and lemon wedges, to garnish

serves *four*
preparation time *15 minutes*

method

1 Put the crabmeat, spring onions and herbs in a bowl and mix.
2 In a separate bowl, mix together the mayonnaise and yoghurt, then add to the crab mixture and stir. Season to taste with salt and pepper.
3 Halve the avocados lengthways and remove the stones. Place each half on a serving plate and brush the cut surfaces with a little lemon juice to prevent discoloration.
4 Pile the crab mixture into the avocado halves. Garnish with a sprinkling of paprika and the lemon wedges, and serve with fingers of lightly buttered wholemeal bread or toast.

chicken *and* mixed pepper stir-fry

Olive oil is a valuable source of mono-unsaturated fat, and the peppers are rich in vitamin C, which promotes iron absorption and maintains healthy blood vessels.

ingredients

- 1tbsp olive oil
- 1 large clove garlic, finely chopped
- 2.5cm (1in) piece of fresh root ginger, peeled and finely chopped
- 350g (12oz) skinless, boneless chicken breast, cut into strips
- 1 red pepper (capsicum), seeded and sliced
- 1 yellow pepper (capsicum), seeded and sliced
- 1 green pepper (capsicum), seeded and sliced

- 1 courgette (zucchini), thinly sliced diagonally
- 1 leek, washed and thinly sliced
- 115g (4oz) mangetout (snowpeas)
- 2–3tsp cajun seasoning or Chinese 5-spice powder
- 2tbsp dry sherry
- 1tbsp light soy sauce
- sea salt
- freshly ground black pepper
- sesame seeds, to garnish

serves *four*
preparation time *20 minutes*
cooking time *8–10 minutes*

method

1 Heat the oil in a non-stick wok or large frying pan. Add the garlic and ginger, and stir-fry over a high heat for 30 seconds.

2 Add the chicken and stir-fry for 1–2 minutes, until coloured all over. Add the peppers, courgettes, leeks and mangetout, and stir-fry for a further 2–3 minutes.

3 Add the cajun seasoning or 5-spice powder, sherry, soy sauce, salt and pepper, and stir-fry for another 3–4 minutes, until the chicken and vegetables are cooked and tender.

4 Sprinkle with the sesame seeds and serve with rice noodles.

baked bananas *with* cinnamon

Bananas make this dessert rich in potassium, a mineral instrumental in maintaining proper muscle function and blood pressure.

ingredients

- 4tbsp unsweetened orange juice
- 4tbsp honey
- 2tbsp rum
- 4 firm, ripe bananas
- 2 cinnamon sticks, broken in half

serves *four*
preparation time *10 minutes*
cooking time *30 minutes*

method

1 Preheat the oven to 180°C/350°F/gas mark 4.

2 Put the orange juice, honey and rum in a small bowl and mix well.

3 Peel the bananas and slice each in half lengthways. Place in a shallow, ovenproof dish and add the cinnamon sticks.

4 Pour over the orange juice mixture and turn the bananas over to coat.

5 Cover the dish with foil and bake for about 30 minutes, until the bananas are softened.

6 Remove and discard the cinnamon sticks. Serve the bananas on warmed serving plates with the sauce spooned over.

7 Add a dollop of crème fraîche, light sour cream or plain yoghurt, or a scoop of home-made yoghurt ice.

foods for teeth *and* bones

CALCIUM IS A CRUCIAL *component of bones and teeth. The best food sources are dairy products, canned fish (with bones) and some dark-green leafy vegetables. Vitamin D, found in oily fish, promotes the absorption of calcium into the bloodstream.*

Magnesium is also vital for healthy bones and teeth. Good sources include bananas, brown rice, fish, green vegetables, nuts, pasta and pulses. Beta carotene, which the body can convert to vitamin A, is found in dark leafy vegetables, carrots and yellow or orange fruits.

roasted baby vegetables

This delicious and nutritious starter easy to make. A grated cheese topping gives the vegetables a calcium boost for healthy bones and teeth.

ingredients

- 280g (10oz) baby courgettes (zucchini)
- 280g (10oz) baby aubergines (eggplants)
- 225g (8oz) baby sweetcorn
- 225g (8oz) baby (pickling) onions or shallots (French shallots), halved
- 225g (8oz) button mushrooms
- 2 cloves garlic, thinly sliced
- 2tbsp olive oil
- 250g (9oz) cherry tomatoes
- 1tbsp each chopped fresh thyme and parsley
- salt and black pepper
- 3–4tbsp French dressing (see recipe on page 21)

serves *four to six*
preparation time *10 minutes*
cooking time *30 minutes*

method

1 Preheat the oven to 220°C/425°F/gas mark 7.
2 Put the courgettes, aubergines, sweetcorn, onions or shallots, mushrooms and garlic in a large roasting tin. Drizzle over the oil and toss well.
3 Bake for 20 minutes, stirring once or twice.
4 Add the tomatoes, herbs and seasoning, and stir to mix. Bake for a further 5–10 minutes, until the vegetables are cooked and are just beginning to brown at the edges.
5 Sprinkle the vegetables with the French dressing and toss lightly. Serve with wholemeal bread or rolls.

variations

- *Top the cooked vegetables with grated Cheddar or mozzarella cheese and place under a hot grill until melted.*
- *Use chopped fresh basil or marjoram instead of thyme.*

melon *and* kiwifruit cocktail

This light and tasty starter can be served on its own or with oatcakes or crispbread. Kiwifruit are a good source of vitamin C and potassium, vital for bones.

ingredients

- 1 medium-sized orange- or yellow-fleshed melon
- 4 kiwifruit
- 150ml (¼ pint) unsweetened apple or grape juice
- 1–2tbsp fruit liqueur or brandy
- fresh mint sprigs, to garnish

serves *four*
preparation time *10 minutes, plus 1 hour standing time*

method

1 Halve the melon, and remove and discard the seeds. Peel the melon, chop the flesh into bite-sized pieces and put into a bowl.
2 Peel the kiwifruit and dice the flesh. Add to the chopped melon and stir.
3 Mix together the apple or grape juice and liqueur or brandy. Pour over the fruit and stir to mix. Cover and set aside for about 1 hour, to allow the flavours to blend.
4 Spoon the fruit and juices into four serving dishes and garnish with the mint sprigs.
5 Serve with oatcakes or crispbread.

variations

- *Use a melon baller and make balls instead of cubes.*
- *Use a pineapple instead of a melon.*
- *Use 225g (8oz) strawberries, halved, instead of the kiwifruit.*

hot spinach soufflé

This savoury soufflé will be enjoyed by all the family. Spinach is a good source of magnesium, beta carotene and folate.

ingredients

- 1tbsp finely grated fresh Parmesan cheese
- 450g (1lb) spinach leaves, washed and chopped
- 25g (1oz) butter
- 25g (1oz) plain wholemeal flour
- 250ml (9fl oz) milk
- 4 medium eggs, separated, plus 1 extra egg white
- 115g (4oz) Cheddar cheese, grated
- pinch of cayenne pepper
- sea salt
- freshly ground black pepper

serves *four to six*
preparation time *20 minutes*
cooking time *30–45 minutes*

method

1 Preheat the oven to 190°C/375°F/gas mark 5.
2 Lightly grease a 1.5 litre (2¾ pint) soufflé dish. Sprinkle the dish with Parmesan cheese and set aside.
3 Cook the spinach in a little boiling water until just cooked. Drain well, then chop finely.
4 Put the butter, flour and milk in a saucepan and heat gently, whisking until the sauce comes to the boil and thickens. Simmer for 2 minutes, stirring.
5 Stir in the spinach and cool.
6 Gradually beat in the egg yolks and 85g (3oz) cheese. Add the cayenne pepper and seasoning.
7 Whisk the egg whites until stiff, then fold into the spinach mixture.
8 Spoon into the soufflé dish and sprinkle with the remaining cheese. Place on a baking tray and bake for 30–45 minutes, until well risen, golden brown and just set.
9 Serve with a mixed salad or wholemeal bread.

grilled mackerel *with* rosemary

Lemon and rosemary add flavour to char-grilled mackerel in this delicious recipe. Vitamin D, which occurs naturally in oily fish, promotes the absorption of calcium from the gut to the bloodstream.

ingredients

- 4 fresh mackerel, each weighing about 280–350g (10–12oz), cleaned, and with bones and heads removed
- juice of 2 lemons
- 2tbsp olive oil
- 2tbsp chopped fresh rosemary
- sea salt
- freshly ground black pepper
- fresh rosemary sprigs, to garnish

serves *four*
preparation time *5 minutes, plus 1–2 hours marinating time*
cooking time *10–12 minutes*

method

1 Make two or three diagonal cuts on both sides of each fish. Place in a shallow, non-metallic dish.

2 Put the lemon juice, oil, rosemary and seasoning in a small bowl and whisk. Pour the mixture over the fish and turn to coat completely. Cover and refrigerate for 1–2 hours.

3 Preheat the barbecue coals or grill to medium. Place the mackerel on a grill rack and cook for 10–12 minutes, until the flesh just flakes when tested with a fork. Turn during cooking and brush regularly with the marinade to prevent the fish drying out.

4 Garnish with the rosemary sprigs and serve with baked potatoes and home-made coleslaw.

variations

- *Use sardines instead of mackerel.*
- *Use lime or orange juice instead of lemon.*
- *Use fresh thyme instead of rosemary.*

salmon *and* asparagus risotto

Salmon and asparagus add extra flavour and nutrients to this tasty risotto. Salmon and brown rice both provide magnesium, a crucial mineral for maintaining healthy bones and teeth.

ingredients

- 1tbsp olive oil
- 1 onion, chopped
- 2 cloves garlic, finely chopped
- 225g (8oz) mushrooms, sliced
- 225g (8oz) long grain brown rice
- 300ml (½ pint) dry white wine
- 425ml (¾ pint) boiling vegetable stock (see recipe on page 20)
- 280g (10oz) fresh asparagus, chopped into 2.5cm (1in) lengths
- 400g (14oz) can salmon in water, drained and flaked
- 2tbsp chopped fresh tarragon
- sea salt
- freshly ground black pepper

serves *four*
preparation time *15 minutes*
cooking time *40 minutes*

method

1 Heat the oil in a saucepan. Add the onion and garlic, and cook for 5 minutes, stirring occasionally.

2 Add the mushrooms and rice. Cook for 1 minute, stirring.

3 Add the wine and a little stock. Bring to the boil, reduce the heat and simmer, uncovered, until almost all the liquid has been absorbed.

4 Continue gradually adding the stock until the rice is cooked, stirring occasionally.

5 Meanwhile, steam the asparagus over a saucepan of boiling water for 8–10 minutes, until tender. Drain well and keep warm.

6 Stir the asparagus, salmon and tarragon into the risotto. Season to taste, and cook gently until the salmon is hot.

7 Serve with a mixed tomato and pepper (capsicum) salad.

variations

- *Use canned tuna instead of salmon.*
- *Use coriander instead of tarragon.*
- *Use courgettes (zucchini) instead of mushrooms.*

lamb *and* apricot pilaf

This fruity lamb pilaf is sure to become a favourite with all the family. Lamb, rice and cashews provide magnesium, and dried fruits, such as apricots, provide boron, essential elements for strong bones and teeth.

ingredients

- 1tbsp olive oil
- 350g (12oz) lean lamb, cut into 2.5cm (1in) cubes
- 1 onion, chopped
- 1 red pepper (capsicum), seeded and diced
- 1 clove garlic, crushed
- 2.5cm (1in) piece of root ginger, peeled and finely chopped
- 2tsp ground cumin
- 1tsp ground coriander
- 225g (8oz) long grain brown basmati rice
- 450ml (16fl oz) vegetable stock (see recipe on page 20)
- 150ml (¼ pint) red wine
- sea salt
- freshly ground black pepper
- 115g (4oz) ready-to-eat dried apricots, chopped
- 55–85g (2–3oz) unsalted cashew nuts
- fresh coriander sprigs, to garnish

serves *four*
preparation time *15 minutes*
cooking time *40–45 minutes*

method

1 Heat the oil in a large saucepan. Add the lamb and cook until browned all over. Remove the lamb from the pan using a slotted spoon, set aside and keep warm.

2 Add the onion, pepper, garlic and ginger to the pan and cook for 3 minutes, stirring occasionally.

3 Add the ground spices and cook for 1 minute, stirring.

4 Return the lamb to the pan, add the rice, stock, wine and seasoning, and stir. Cover, bring to the boil, then reduce the heat and simmer for 15 minutes, stirring occasionally.

5 Stir in the apricots. Return to the boil, cover and simmer for a further 15–20 minutes, until the lamb is cooked and almost all the liquid has been absorbed.

6 Fold in the cashew nuts, then spoon into a warmed serving dish. Garnish with the coriander sprigs.

7 Serve with cooked fresh vegetables, such as spinach and green beans.

variations

- *Use large raisins instead of apricots.*
- *Use flaked or whole almonds instead of cashew nuts.*

freezing instructions

Allow to cool completely, then transfer to a rigid, freezeproof container. Cover, seal and label. Freeze for up to 3 months. Defrost completely, then reheat gently in a saucepan until piping hot, adding a little extra stock if necessary.

pan-fried liver *with* mushrooms *and* sage

Succulent lamb's liver combines wonderfully with mushrooms and fresh sage. Lamb's liver contains many nutrients, including vitamin A – an essential nutrient for healthy bones and teeth.

ingredients

- 15g (½oz) butter
- 1tbsp olive oil
- 1 onion, sliced
- 450g (1lb) lamb's liver, cut into thin strips
- 225g (8oz) small button mushrooms
- 6tbsp port or red wine
- 1tbsp chopped fresh sage
- sea salt
- freshly ground black pepper
- fresh sage leaves, to garnish

serves *four to six*
preparation time *10–15 minutes*
cooking time *20 minutes*

method

1 Heat the butter and oil in a large non-stick frying pan until the butter is melted. Add the onion and cook gently for about 10 minutes, stirring occasionally, until the onion is softened.

2 Add the liver, mushrooms and port or wine. Cook over a medium to low heat for about 10 minutes, until the liver is just cooked, stirring occasionally.

3 Stir in the chopped sage and season to taste.

4 Garnish with the sage leaves.

5 Serve with brown rice and cooked fresh vegetables, such as peas and carrots.

variations

- *Use lamb's kidneys instead of liver.*
- *Use sherry or brandy instead of port or red wine.*
- *Use fresh thyme instead of sage.*

country chicken *and* barley casserole

This wholesome casserole makes a hearty, warming dish for winter days. Wholegrains such as barley contain magnesium, which helps to strengthen bones and teeth.

ingredients

- 1tbsp olive oil
- 4 skinless chicken breasts
- 350g (12oz) button onions, peeled
- 2 leeks, washed and sliced
- 225g (8oz) baby (Dutch) carrots
- 225g (8oz) button mushrooms
- 225g (8oz) celeriac, diced
- 55g (2oz) pearl barley
- 400g (14oz) can tomatoes, chopped
- 2tbsp tomato purée (paste)
- 425ml (¾ pint) chicken stock (see recipe on page 20)
- 300ml (½ pint) dry white wine
- 1 bouquet garni
- sea salt
- freshly ground black pepper
- fresh herb sprigs, to garnish

serves *four*
preparation time *15 minutes*
cooking time *1½–2 hours*

method

1 Preheat the oven to 180°C/350°F/gas mark 4.

2 Heat the oil in a large flameproof and ovenproof casserole dish. Add the chicken and cook until browned.

3 Stir in all the remaining ingredients. Bring to the boil, cover and bake in the oven for 1½ hours. Remove the bouquet garni.

4 Garnish with the herb sprigs.

5 Serve with potatoes and broccoli or cauliflower florets.

variations

- *Use turkey instead of chicken.*
- *Use swede instead of celeriac.*
- *Use green split peas instead of pearl barley.*

freezing instructions

Allow to cool completely, then transfer to a rigid, freezeproof container. Cover, seal and label. Freeze for up to 3 months. Defrost thoroughly, and reheat gently in a moderate oven until piping hot.

tofu *and* vegetable kebabs

The whole family will enjoy these tasty vegetarian kebabs made of marinated tofu and vegetables. For a rich source of calcium, choose tofu that is made with calcium chloride.

ingredients

- 3tbsp olive oil
- finely grated rind and juice of 1 lemon
- 1 clove garlic, crushed
- 1tsp each ground cumin and hot chilli powder
- 1tbsp chopped fresh mixed herbs
- sea salt
- freshly ground black pepper
- 280g (10oz) tofu, cut into small cubes
- 4 shallots (French shallots), halved
- 1 red pepper (capsicum), seeded and cut into 8 chunks
- 1 courgette (zucchini), cut into 16 thin slices
- 16 button mushrooms
- 16 cherry tomatoes

serves *four (two kebabs per serving)*
preparation time *10 minutes, plus 30 minutes marinating time*
cooking time *8 minutes*

method

1 Put the olive oil, lemon rind and juice, garlic, spices, herbs and seasoning in a bowl and whisk.
2 Place the tofu in a shallow, non-metallic dish, pour over the oil mixture and toss. Cover and set aside for 30 minutes.
3 Preheat the grill to high. Thread the tofu and vegetables on to four long or eight short skewers, dividing the ingredients evenly.
4 Place the kebabs on a rack in a grill pan and grill for 3–4 minutes on each side, until lightly browned, turning frequently. Brush with the marinade mixture regularly during cooking.
5 Serve the kebabs on a bed of brown rice with a salad.

variations

- *To make a tofu and vegetable stir-fry, marinate the tofu as directed. Heat a little olive oil in a non-stick wok or frying pan, add the tofu and vegetables and stir-fry for 6–8 minutes. Add the marinade, stir-fry for 2 minutes, then serve hot.*

spiced vegetable couscous

A spicy vegetable sauce served on a bed of hot couscous creates a nutritious appetising meal. Leafy green vegetables, such as broccoli, contain calcium and magnesium, both good for bones.

ingredients

- 2tbsp olive oil
- 1 large onion, sliced
- 2 cloves garlic, finely chopped
- 2 courgettes (zucchini), sliced
- 175g (6oz) broccoli florets
- 225g (8oz) mushrooms, sliced
- 2 carrots, thinly sliced
- 1 red pepper (capsicum), seeded and sliced
- 1tbsp ground mixed spices such as coriander, cumin, chilli and allspice
- 600ml (1 pint) vegetable stock (see recipe on page 20)
- sea salt
- freshly ground black pepper
- 225g (8oz) frozen peas
- 2–3tbsp cornflour
- 350g (12oz) quick-cook (instant) couscous
- fresh herb sprigs, to garnish

serves *four to six*
preparation time *15 minutes*
cooking time *25–30 minutes*

method

1 Heat 1tbsp oil in a saucepan. Add all the fresh vegetables and cook gently for 5 minutes.
2 Add the ground spices and cook for 1 minute, stirring.
3 Add the stock, seasoning and peas, and stir.
4 Blend the cornflour with 4–5tbsp water and stir into the vegetable mixture. Bring to the boil, stirring continuously, until the mixture thickens slightly.
5 Reduce the heat, cover and simmer for 15–20 minutes, until the vegetables are tender.
6 Soak and cook the couscous according to the directions.
7 Stir in the remaining oil, then spoon the couscous onto warmed serving plates. Spoon the vegetable mixture on top. Garnish with the herb sprigs.

variations

- *Choose your own mixture of fresh and frozen vegetables.*
- *Serve the sauce with brown rice or pasta instead of couscous.*

fragrant fruit salad

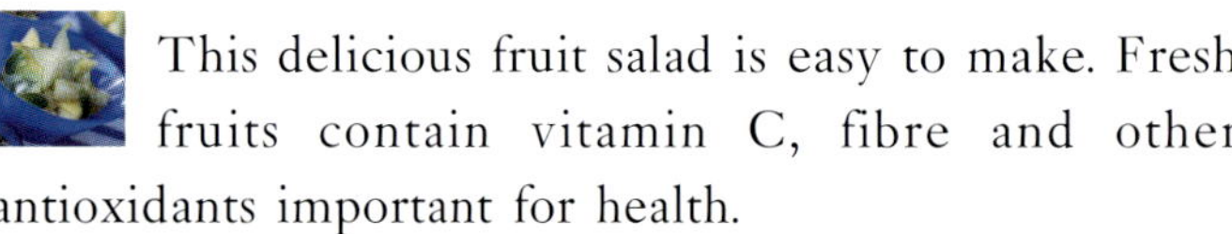

This delicious fruit salad is easy to make. Fresh fruits contain vitamin C, fibre and other antioxidants important for health.

ingredients

- 1 small pineapple
- 1 ripe mango
- 1 carambola (star fruit)
- 3 kiwifruit
- 200ml (7fl oz) unsweetened apple juice
- 200ml (7fl oz) unsweetened orange juice
- 2tbsp ginger wine
- 2tbsp honey (optional)
- fresh mint sprigs, to decorate

serves *four to six*
preparation time *15 minutes, plus 1 hour standing time*

method

1 Peel, core and chop the pineapple. Peel, stone and chop the mango. Place in a bowl.
2 Slice the carambola and peel and slice the kiwifruit. Add to the bowl and stir to mix.
3 Mix together the fruit juices, ginger wine and honey, if using. Pour over the fruit and stir gently.
4 Cover and leave to stand at room temperature for 1 hour before serving to allow the flavours to blend.
5 Spoon into bowls to serve and decorate with the mint sprigs.
6 Serve with home-made yoghurt ice or plain yoghurt.

variations

- *Use other fresh fruit mixtures, such as apples, pears, cherries, peaches and apricots.*
- *Use unsweetened grape or pineapple juice instead of apple or orange juice.*
- *For extra calcium, top with a teaspoon of sesame seeds.*

fruity breakfast muffins

You can't beat the aroma and flavour of these raspberry muffins, ideal for a breakfast-time treat. Raspberries are a good source of vitamin C, vital for healthy gums and teeth.

ingredients

- 200g (7oz) plain wholemeal flour
- 1tbsp baking powder
- pinch of salt
- 115g (4oz) small fresh raspberries
- 55g (2oz) butter, melted
- 55g (2oz) light brown sugar
- 1 medium egg, beaten
- 200ml (7fl oz) milk

makes *nine muffins*
preparation time *20 minutes*
cooking time *20 minutes*

method

1 Preheat the oven to 200°C/400°F/gas mark 6. Line nine muffin tins with paper cases.
2 Put the flour, baking powder and salt in a large bowl and stir in the raspberries.
3 Mix the melted butter, sugar, egg and milk in a separate bowl, then pour over the flour mixture.
4 Gently fold the ingredients together, and spoon the mixture into the prepared muffin cases, filling each case two-thirds full.
5 Bake for 20 minutes until golden brown.
6 Transfer to a wire rack to cool. Serve plain, or split and spread with a little butter, preserve, honey or fruit curd.

variations

- *Use other fresh or dried fruit instead of raspberries.*
- *Add the finely grated rind of 1 lemon or orange, or 1–2tsp ground mixed spice, cinnamon or ginger, to the mixture before baking.*

summer strawberry yoghurt ice

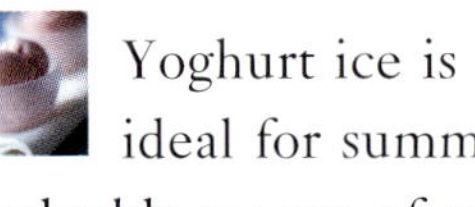

Yoghurt ice is a delicious and nutritious dessert, ideal for summertime eating alfresco. Yoghurt is a valuable source of calcium, a fundamental mineral for healthy bones and teeth.

ingredients

- 450g (1lb) strawberries
- 55g (2oz) brown sugar
- 300ml (½ pint) plain yoghurt
- 300ml (½ pint) strawberry yoghurt
- fresh mint sprigs, to decorate

serves *six*
preparation time *10 minutes, plus freezing time*

method

1 Put the strawberries in a food processor and blend until smooth. Add the sugar and yoghurts, and blend until well mixed.
2 Pour the mixture into a chilled, shallow, plastic container. Cover and freeze for 1½–2 hours, or until the mixture is mushy. Spoon into a bowl and mash with a fork to break up the ice crystals. Return the mixture to the container, cover and freeze until firm.
3 Transfer the yoghurt ice to the refrigerator 30 minutes before serving to allow it to soften a little. Serve in scoops, decorated with the mint sprigs.
4 Serve with fresh fruit, such as raspberries or sliced peaches.

variations

- *Replace the strawberries with blackberries and the strawberry yoghurt with raspberry yoghurt.*
- *Use honey instead of sugar.*

freezing instructions

The yoghurt ice will keep for up to 3 months in the freezer.

bred *in the* bone

TO ENSURE YOU *don't go weak in the knees, here is a scrumptious selection of recipes to help nourish and strengthen your bones and teeth. This mouthwatering menu contains all those essential vitamins and minerals that help to maintain strong bones and teeth.*

hot spinach soufflé

Excellent for fighting the damaging effects of free radicals, spinach is a good source of magnesium, beta carotene and vitamin C – essential nutrients for building strong bones and teeth.

ingredients

- 1tbsp finely grated fresh Parmesan cheese
- 450g (1lb) spinach leaves, washed and chopped
- 25g (1oz) butter
- 25g (1oz) plain wholemeal flour
- 250ml (9fl oz) milk
- 4 medium eggs, separated, plus 1 extra egg white
- 115g (4oz) Cheddar cheese, grated
- pinch of cayenne pepper
- sea salt
- freshly ground black pepper

serves *four to six*
preparation time *20 minutes*
cooking time *30–45 minutes*

method

1 Preheat the oven to 190°C/375°F/gas mark 5.
2 Lightly grease a 1.5 litre (2¾ pint) soufflé dish. Sprinkle the dish with Parmesan cheese and set aside.
3 Cook the spinach in a little boiling water until just cooked. Drain well, then chop finely.
4 Put the butter, flour and milk in a saucepan and heat gently, whisking until the sauce comes to the boil and thickens. Simmer for 2 minutes, stirring.
5 Stir in the spinach and cool.
6 Gradually beat in the egg yolks and 85g (3oz) cheese. Add the cayenne pepper and seasoning.
7 Whisk the egg whites until stiff, then fold into the spinach mixture.
8 Spoon into the soufflé dish and sprinkle with the remaining cheese. Place on a baking tray and bake for 30–45 minutes, until well risen, golden brown and just set.
9 Serve with a mixed salad or wholemeal bread.

salmon *and* asparagus risotto

Both salmon and brown rice are good sources of the magnesium needed for healthy bones and teeth.

ingredients

- 1tbsp olive oil
- 1 onion, chopped
- 2 cloves garlic, finely chopped
- 225g (8oz) mushrooms, sliced
- 225g (8oz) long grain brown rice
- 300ml (½ pint) dry white wine
- 425ml (¾ pint) boiling vegetable stock (see recipe on page 20)
- 280g (10oz) fresh asparagus, chopped into 2.5cm (1in) lengths
- 400g (14oz) can salmon in water, drained and flaked
- 2tbsp chopped fresh tarragon
- sea salt
- freshly ground black pepper

serves *four*
preparation time *15 minutes*
cooking time *40 minutes*

method

1 Heat the oil in a saucepan. Add the onion and garlic, and cook for 5 minutes, stirring occasionally.
2 Add the mushrooms and rice. Cook for 1 minute, stirring.
3 Add the wine and a little stock. Bring to the boil, reduce the heat and simmer, uncovered, until almost all the liquid has been absorbed.
4 Continue gradually adding the stock until the rice is cooked, stirring occasionally.
5 Meanwhile, steam the asparagus over a saucepan of boiling water for 8–10 minutes, until tender. Drain well and keep warm.
6 Stir the asparagus, salmon and tarragon into the risotto. Season to taste, and cook gently until the salmon is hot.
7 Serve with a mixed tomato and pepper (capsicum) salad.

fragrant fruit salad

A juicy way to round off this bone-strengthening menu – these fresh fruits provide plenty of vitamin C, good for teeth, bones and gums.

ingredients

- 1 small pineapple
- 1 ripe mango
- 1 carambola (star fruit)
- 3 kiwifruit
- 200ml (7fl oz) unsweetened apple juice
- 200ml (7fl oz) unsweetened orange juice
- 2tbsp ginger wine
- 2tbsp honey (optional)
- fresh mint sprigs, to decorate

serves *four to six*
preparation time *15 minutes, plus 1 hour standing time*

method

1 Peel, core and chop the pineapple. Peel, stone and chop the mango. Place in a bowl.
2 Slice the carambola and peel and slice the kiwifruit. Add to the bowl and stir to mix.
3 Mix together the fruit juices, ginger wine and honey, if using. Pour over the fruit and stir gently.
4 Cover and leave to stand at room temperature for 1 hour before serving to allow the flavours to blend.
5 Spoon into bowls to serve and decorate with the mint sprigs.
6 Serve with home-made yoghurt ice or plain yoghurt.

flexibility *foods*

For joint mobility, antioxidants, such as beta vitamin C and beta carotene, are important – good sources include green, yellow, orange and red fruits and vegetables. Selenium may also be a vital nutrient for healthy joints. The best sources are grains, seafood, fresh fish, meat, eggs, lamb's liver and kidneys, onions and Brazil nuts. A deficiency of boron – found in fruits, vegetables, pulses and nuts – may aggravate symptoms of arthritis. Vitamin A, which the body can make from beta carotene, is important in the manufacture of chemicals that are a vital component of the fluid that lubricates joints.

red pepper soup

This colourful soup makes an ideal light starter and is delicious topped with crisp wholemeal croutons. Red peppers (capsicums) provide beta carotene (for vitamin A) and vitamin C; the latter is thought to help joint mobility.

ingredients

- 1tbsp olive oil
- 8 shallots (French shallots), finely chopped
- 1 large clove garlic, crushed
- 3 large red peppers (capsicums), seeded and diced
- 450g (1lb) tomatoes, chopped
- 850ml (1½ pints) vegetable stock (see recipe on page 20)
- 2tbsp chopped fresh basil
- sea salt and ground black pepper
- 2tbsp crème fraîche or light sour cream (optional)
- fresh basil sprigs, to garnish

serves *four*
preparation time *10 minutes*
cooking time *25–30 minutes*

method

1 Heat the oil in a large saucepan. Add the shallots, garlic and peppers, and cook for 5 minutes.

2 Add the tomatoes and stock. Cover, bring to the boil, then reduce the heat and simmer for 20–25 minutes, until the vegetables are tender.

3 Cool slightly, then purée in a blender or food processor until smooth. Press the mixture through a sieve and discard the pulp.

4 Return the soup to the rinsed-out saucepan, stir in the chopped basil and seasoning, and reheat gently until piping hot. Stir in the crème fraîche or light sour cream.

5 Ladle into warmed soup bowls, garnish with the basil sprigs and serve with wholemeal rolls.

variations

- *Use an onion instead of shallots.*
- *Use 400g (14oz) can tomatoes, chopped, instead of fresh tomatoes.*
- *Use chopped fresh coriander or parsley instead of basil.*

freezing instructions

Allow to cool completely, then transfer to a rigid, freezeproof container. Cover, seal and label. Freeze for up to 3 months. Defrost, and reheat gently in a saucepan until piping hot.

seafood brochettes

These tasty brochettes make a great summertime dish. A deficiency of the trace element selenium, found in seafood, has been linked to rheumatoid arthritis. The omega-6 fatty acids in the olive oil marinade are also thought to improve joint mobility.

ingredients

- 12 shelled tiger (or king) prawns
- 12 shelled scallops
- 225g (8oz) salmon fillet, cut into 2.5cm (1in) cubes
- 225g (8oz) firm white fish fillet, such as haddock or gemfish, cut into 2.5cm (1in) cubes
- 1 small red pepper (capsicum), seeded and cut into 8 pieces
- 1 small yellow pepper (capsicum), seeded and cut into 8 pieces
- 12 cherry tomatoes
- 4tbsp olive oil
- finely grated rind and juice of 2 limes
- 1tsp Chinese 5-spice powder
- sea salt
- freshly ground black pepper

serves *four to six*
preparation time *10 minutes, plus 2–3 hours marinating time*
cooking time *8–10 minutes*

method

1 Thread the mixed seafood and vegetables onto four or six skewers, dividing the ingredients evenly. Put the skewers in a shallow, non-metallic dish.

2 Put the oil, lime rind and juice, spice and seasoning in a bowl and whisk until well mixed. Drizzle over the brochettes, then turn the brochettes to coat completely. Cover and leave to marinate in the refrigerator for 2–3 hours.

3 Preheat the grill to high. Place the brochettes on a rack in a grill pan and grill for 8–10 minutes, until cooked, turning occasionally. Brush frequently with the marinade during cooking.

4 Serve with wholemeal bread rolls.

variations

- *Use button mushrooms instead of cherry tomatoes.*
- *Use lemons instead of limes.*

green vegetable frittata

Frittatas are quick and easy to make for a filling starter or snack. Green vegetables contain beta carotene (for vitamin A) and vitamin C as well as boron, which is an important bone mineral.

ingredients

- 175g (6oz) small broccoli florets
- 115g (4oz) frozen peas
- 2tbsp olive oil
- 1 onion, chopped
- 225g (8oz) cold boiled potatoes, diced
- 55g (2oz) spinach, shredded
- 6 medium eggs
- 2tbsp chopped fresh mixed herbs
- sea salt
- freshly ground black pepper
- 55g (2oz) Cheddar cheese, grated

serves *four to six*
preparation time *10 minutes*
cooking time *25–30 minutes*

method

1 Cook the broccoli and peas in a saucepan of boiling water for 4 minutes. Drain well.

2 Heat the oil in a large non-stick frying pan, add the onion and cook gently for 10 minutes.

3 Add the potatoes and spinach and cook for 5 minutes.

4 Beat the eggs and add the broccoli, peas, herbs and seasoning. Pour over the vegetables in the pan, spreading the mixture evenly.

5 Cook over a medium heat until the eggs are beginning to set and the frittata is golden underneath.

6 Preheat the grill to medium.

7 Sprinkle the cheese over the top and grill until it has melted and the top is golden brown.

8 Cut into wedges and serve with a mixed tomato, pepper (capsicum) and onion salad.

variations

- *Use sliced courgettes (zucchini) instead of broccoli florets.*
- *Use 6 shallots (French shallots) instead of the onion.*

pan-fried citrus trout

These trout fillets, marinated in a citrus juice and served with a selection of cooked fresh vegetables, make a simple and delicious meal. Fresh fish contains selenium, an essential nutrient for healthy joints.

ingredients

- 8 trout fillets, each weighing about 85g (3oz)
- pared rind and juice of 1 large lemon
- juice of 1 orange
- 2 cloves garlic, crushed
- sea salt
- freshly ground black pepper
- 1tbsp olive oil
- 15g (½oz) butter
- 1tbsp chopped fresh parsley
- 1tbsp chopped fresh basil

serves *four*
preparation time *10 minutes, plus 1 hour marinating time*
cooking time *10 minutes*

method

1 Put the fish fillets in a shallow, non-metallic dish.
2 Mix together the lemon rind and juice, orange juice, garlic and seasoning, and pour over the fish. Turn the fish over in the marinade. Cover and leave in the refrigerator to marinate for 1 hour.
3 Heat the oil and butter in a large non-stick frying pan until the butter is melted. Using a slotted spoon, remove the fish from the marinade and add to the pan.
4 Cook for 2–3 minutes on each side, until the flesh just flakes when tested with a fork.
5 Using a fish slice, put the fish on a warmed serving plate. Cover and keep hot.
6 Add the marinade to the pan, discarding the lemon rind. Bring to the boil and boil rapidly for a few minutes, stirring occasionally, until the sauce has reduced and thickened slightly.
7 Pour the sauce over the fish, sprinkle with the fresh herbs and serve with cooked fresh vegetables, such as new potatoes, spinach and baby (Dutch) carrots.

variation

- *Use chopped fresh coriander instead of basil.*

prawn *and* broccoli stir-fry

Stir-frying is a quick, easy and nutritious way of cooking vegetables. Prawns provide a host of vitamins and minerals, as well as protein. Broccoli contains carotenoids, vitamin C and boron, all nutrients that help keep joints healthy and mobile.

ingredients

- 225g (8oz) small broccoli florets
- 2tsp cornflour
- 4tbsp unsweetened apple juice
- 1tbsp dry sherry
- 1tbsp light soy sauce
- 1tbsp honey
- 2tsp tomato purée (paste)
- salt
- freshly ground black pepper
- 1tbsp olive oil
- 1 clove garlic, finely chopped
- 2.5cm (1in) piece of fresh root ginger, peeled and finely chopped
- 1 carrot, cut into matchstick (julienne) strips
- 2 courgettes (zucchini), cut into matchstick (julienne) strips
- 350g (12oz) cooked, shelled prawns
- 115g (4oz) beansprouts

serves *four to six*
preparation time *15 minutes*
cooking time *8–10 minutes*

method

1 Cook the broccoli in a saucepan of boiling water for 2 minutes. Drain well and keep warm.

2 In a small bowl, blend the cornflour with the apple juice. Stir in the sherry, soy sauce, honey, tomato purée and seasoning. Set to one side.

3 Heat the oil in a non-stick wok or large frying pan. Add the garlic and ginger, and stir-fry over a high heat for 30 seconds. Add the carrot and courgettes, and stir-fry for 2–3 minutes.

4 Add the broccoli, prawns and beansprouts, and stir-fry for a further 2–3 minutes. Add the cornflour mixture, stir until the mixture thickens, then stir-fry for a further 1–2 minutes.

5 Serve with a mixture of brown and wild rice.

variation

- *Use cauliflower florets instead of broccoli.*

braised liver *with* fresh thyme

Lamb's liver braised with fresh wild mushrooms and thyme makes a wonderfully tender and nutritious dish. Lamb's liver provides vitamin A and selenium, an antioxidant that is important for joints. The olive oil used for frying provides omega-6 fatty acids, which are thought to aid joint mobility.

ingredients

- 2tbsp olive oil
- 1 large onion, sliced
- 450g (1lb) lamb's liver, thinly sliced
- 175g (6oz) mixed fresh wild mushrooms, such as shiitake and oyster, sliced
- 350g (12oz) tomatoes, skinned, seeded and cut into thin strips
- 150ml (¼ pint) red wine or dry white wine
- 1tbsp chopped fresh thyme
- sea salt
- freshly ground black pepper
- fresh thyme sprigs, to garnish

serves *four to six*
preparation time *15 minutes*
cooking time *20 minutes*

method

1 Heat the oil in a large non-stick frying pan, add the onion and cook gently for 10 minutes, stirring occasionally, until softened.

2 Add the liver and mushrooms, and cook for 5 minutes, stirring occasionally.

3 Add the tomatoes, wine and chopped thyme. Bring to the boil and simmer for a further 5 minutes, until the liver is cooked, stirring occasionally.

4 Season to taste.

5 Garnish with the thyme sprigs, and serve with potatoes, and braised carrots and celery.

variations

- *Use lamb's kidneys instead of liver.*
- *Use stock instead of red wine.*
- *Use a red (Spanish) onion instead of a standard onion.*

oven-baked turkey *with* mango salsa

These succulent, oven-baked turkey breasts with a fruity salsa are sure to become a family favourite. Mangoes are a good source of carotenoids and vitamin C, both of which help keep joints healthy and mobile.

ingredients

- 4 skinless, boneless turkey breast steaks
- 1tbsp olive oil
- 2tbsp wholegrain mustard
- 2tbsp chopped fresh tarragon
- sea salt
- freshly ground black pepper
- 1 onion, thinly sliced
- juice of 1 large lemon
- fresh herb sprigs, to garnish

for the salsa

- 1 large ripe mango, peeled, stoned and finely chopped
- 55g (2oz) cucumber, finely chopped
- 4 spring onions, finely chopped
- 1tbsp chopped fresh coriander

serves *four*
preparation time *15 minutes, plus 1–2 hours standing time*
cooking time *30–45 minutes*

method

1 First make the salsa. Put the mango, cucumber, spring onions and coriander in a bowl and mix well. Cover and leave to stand at room temperature for 1–2 hours.

2 Preheat the oven to 190°C/375°F/gas mark 5.

3 Cut four pieces of greaseproof paper, each large enough to wrap a steak. Cut three slashes in each steak and place on the paper.

4 Mix together the oil, mustard, tarragon and seasoning in a small bowl. Spread some of the mixture over each steak.

5 Add a few slices of onion, then drizzle lemon juice over the top. Fold the paper over the steaks and twist the edges to secure, making four parcels.

6 Place on a baking tray and bake for 30–45 minutes, until the turkey is cooked and tender.

7 Unwrap the parcels carefully (to avoid getting burnt by steam) and place the turkey on warmed serving plates. Spoon the juices on top and the salsa alongside. Garnish with the herb sprigs.

8 Serve with sautéed potatoes and grilled peppers (capsicums).

variations

- *Use skinless, boneless chicken breasts instead of turkey.*
- *Use a small fresh pineapple instead of a mango.*
- *Use chopped fresh coriander or basil instead of tarragon.*

summer vegetable quiche

This savoury quiche makes an ideal summertime meal or snack. Green vegetables such as broccoli and asparagus provide boron, a trace element that is good for bones and joints.

ingredients

for the pastry

- 175g (6oz) plain wholemeal flour
- pinch of salt
- 85g (3oz) butter, chopped

for the filling

- 55g (2oz) small broccoli florets
- 55g (2oz) asparagus tips
- 1 courgette (zucchini), thinly sliced
- 2 plum (Roma) tomatoes, sliced
- 85g (3oz) Cheddar cheese, grated
- 2 medium eggs
- 150ml (¼ pint) milk
- 1–2tbsp chopped fresh mixed herbs
- sea salt
- freshly ground black pepper

serves *six*
preparation time *15 minutes, plus chilling time*
cooking time *55 minutes*

method

1 Put the flour and salt in a bowl, then lightly rub in the butter until the mixture resembles breadcrumbs. Stir in enough cold water to form a soft dough.

2 Roll the dough out and line a 20cm (8in) flan tin. Cover and chill for 20 minutes.

3 Preheat the oven to 200°C/400°F/gas mark 6.

4 Line the pastry case with non-stick baking paper and fill with baking beans. Place on a baking tray and bake blind for 10 minutes. Remove from the oven and reduce the oven temperature to 180°C/350°F/gas mark 4.

5 Cook the broccoli, asparagus and courgettes in boiling water for 2 minutes. Drain and spoon into the flan case. Top with the tomato slices and sprinkle with the cheese.

6 Beat the eggs, milk, herbs and seasoning together, and pour into the flan case. Bake for about 45 minutes, until golden brown.

7 Serve warm or cold in slices, with baked potatoes and a salad.

bean *and* vegetable chilli

A delicious alternative to meat chilli, this nutritious bean and vegetable chilli, served with brown rice, is ideal for chilly days. Fresh vegetables provide carotenoids, vitamin C and selenium.

ingredients

- 1tbsp olive oil
- 1 onion, sliced
- 1 red pepper (capsicum), seeded and diced
- 2 fresh red chillies, seeded and finely chopped
- 2 cloves garlic, finely chopped
- 2tsp ground coriander
- 2 carrots, sliced
- 225g (8oz) cauliflower florets
- 400g (14oz) can tomatoes, chopped
- 300ml (½ pint) vegetable stock
- 2tbsp sun-dried tomato purée (paste)
- sea salt
- freshly ground black pepper
- 400g (14oz) can each red kidney beans and flageolet beans, rinsed and drained
- 2tbsp cornflour
- fresh coriander sprigs, to garnish

serves *four to six*
preparation time *20 minutes*
cooking time *40–45 minutes*

method

1 Heat the oil in a large saucepan. Add the onion, pepper, chillies, garlic and coriander, and cook gently for 5 minutes.

2 Add the carrots, cauliflower, tomatoes, stock, tomato purée and seasoning, and stir. Cover, bring to the boil, then reduce the heat and simmer for 25 minutes, stirring occasionally.

3 Stir in the beans. Bring back to the boil and cook for a further 10–15 minutes, until the vegetables are tender.

4 Blend the cornflour with 4tbsp water and stir into the bean mixture. Bring to the boil, stirring continuously, until the mixture thickens slightly. Simmer for 2 minutes, stirring.

5 Serve on a bed of herbed brown rice, pasta or couscous and garnish with the coriander sprigs.

variations

- *Use other canned beans, such as black-eye or butter beans.*
- *Use broccoli florets instead of cauliflower florets.*

cherry buckwheat pancakes

These buckwheat pancakes make a substantial dessert served with a delicious, sweet cherry sauce. Cherries are a good source of potassium, which may help to relieve the swelling and pain of gout.

ingredients

for the sauce

- 125ml (4fl oz) red wine
- 55g (2oz) light brown sugar
- 225g (8oz) pitted, fresh, sweet dark cherries
- 2tsp arrowroot
- 2tbsp cherry brandy

for the pancakes

- 55g (2oz) plain wholemeal flour
- 55g (2oz) buckwheat flour
- pinch of salt
- 1 medium egg
- 300ml (½ pint) milk
- sunflower oil, for frying

serves *four (two pancakes each)*
preparation time *25 minutes*
cooking time *15–20 minutes*

method

1 Put the red wine and sugar in a saucepan and heat gently until the sugar has dissolved, stirring continuously. Add the cherries, cover and bring to the boil. Reduce the heat and cook gently for 10 minutes, until the cherries are tender, stirring occasionally.

2 Blend the arrowroot with the cherry brandy and stir into the cherry mixture. Bring to the boil, stirring continuously, until the mixture thickens. Keep the sauce warm while making the pancakes, or serve it cold.

3 To make the pancakes, put the wholemeal flour, buckwheat flour and salt in a bowl, and make a well in the centre. Break in the egg and add a little milk, beating well with a wooden spoon.

4 Gradually beat in the remaining milk, drawing the flour in from the sides, to make a smooth batter.

5 Heat a little oil in an 18cm (7in) non-stick frying pan. Pour in enough batter to thinly coat the base of the pan. Cook until golden brown, then turn and cook on the other side.

6 Transfer the cooked pancake to a warmed plate and keep hot. Repeat with the remaining batter to make eight pancakes, stacking them with greaseproof paper in between.

7 Serve the pancakes hot with warm or cold cherry sauce and crème fraîche, light sour cream or plain yoghurt.

variations

- *Use unsweetened apple juice instead of cherry brandy.*
- *Use plums or raspberries instead of cherries.*
- *Use all wholemeal flour.*

freezing instructions

To freeze the pancakes, beat 1tbsp sunflower oil into the batter, then cook as directed and allow to cool. Interleave the cooked pancakes with lightly oiled non-stick paper or freezer-wrap. Seal in polythene freezer bags or foil and freeze for up to 2 months. Defrost, and reheat each pancake separately in a lightly greased frying pan, about 30 seconds for each side.

mixed berry yoghurt fool

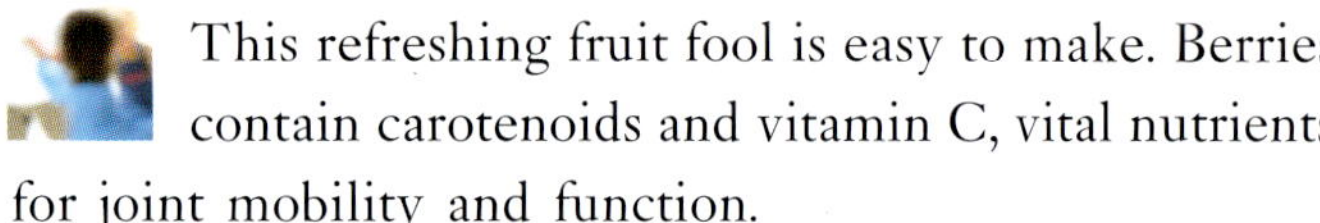

This refreshing fruit fool is easy to make. Berries contain carotenoids and vitamin C, vital nutrients for joint mobility and function.

ingredients

- 700g (1lb 9oz) fresh ripe mixed berries, such as strawberries, raspberries and blackberries
- 4tbsp honey
- 280g (10oz) plain yoghurt
- 6tbsp crème fraîche or light sour cream
- fresh mint sprigs, to decorate

serves *six*
preparation time *15 minutes, plus 30 minutes chilling time*

method

1 Put the berries in a blender or food processor and blend until smooth. Press the purée through a sieve into a bowl, reserving the juice and pulp, and discarding the seeds.

2 Mix the honey with the fruit. Stir the yoghurt and crème fraîche or light sour cream into the fruit mixture until well mixed.

3 Spoon into serving glasses or dishes and chill for 30 minutes before serving. Decorate with the mint sprigs and serve with home-made oat biscuits.

variations

- *Use the same quantity of peeled, stoned ripe mango flesh, instead of berries.*
- *This fruit fool can be set with gelatine. Follow the recipe but before chilling dissolve 1tbsp powdered gelatine in 3tbsp water. Cool slightly, then stir into the berry mixture, mixing well. Pour into serving glasses and chill until set.*

marbled cheesecake

This delicious fruity cheesecake is a real treat for dessert. Blackcurrants are an excellent source of vitamin C and potassium.

ingredients

- 175g (6oz) frozen blackcurrants, cherries or raspberries, defrosted
- 100g (3½oz) light brown sugar
- 85g (3oz) butter, chopped
- 175g (6oz) oat biscuits, crushed
- 1tbsp powdered gelatine
- 115g (4oz) curd (cottage) cheese
- 115g (4oz) plain yoghurt
- 150ml (¼ pint) single (pouring) cream
- finely grated rind and juice of 1 lemon
- 2 medium eggs, separated
- small bunches of redcurrants and fresh mint sprigs, to decorate

serves *six to eight*
preparation time *25 minutes, plus chilling time*

warning

To reduce the risk of salmonella, buy only very fresh eggs in unbroken shells, refrigerate them immediately, and use them as quickly as possible. It is best to avoid uncooked eggs altogether if serving children, elderly people, or anyone with a compromised immune system.

method

1 Purée the fruit and 40g (1½oz) sugar in a food processor. Press through a sieve. Set aside.

2 Melt the butter in a saucepan. Remove from the heat and stir in the biscuit crumbs. Press the mixture over the base of a 20cm (8in), loose-bottomed, deep cake tin. Chill for 30 minutes.

3 Sprinkle the gelatine over 3tbsp water in a small bowl. Soak for a couple of minutes, then place over a pan of simmering water and stir until dissolved.

4 Place the remaining sugar, curd cheese, yoghurt, cream, lemon rind and juice, and egg yolks in a food processor and blend. Add the gelatine and blend until well mixed. Pour into a bowl.

5 Whisk the egg whites until stiff, then fold into the cheese mixture. Pour over the biscuit base.

6 Pour the fruit purée in a thin stream over the cheese mixture and swirl to create a marbled effect. Refrigerate until set.

7 Remove from the tin and decorate with the redcurrants and mint sprigs.

a *moveable* feast

THESE DELICIOUS RECIPES *from the flexibility foods section help supply the vitamins and minerals necessary to keep your joints healthy and mobile. So have your knife and fork at the ready to help keep you mobile and reduce the risk of osteoporosis and arthritis.*

red pepper soup

Kick off with red peppers for a good dose of vitamins A (via beta carotene) and C – both are vital nutrients for joint mobility.

ingredients

- 1tbsp olive oil
- 8 shallots (French shallots), finely chopped
- 1 large clove garlic, crushed
- 3 large red peppers (capsicums), seeded and diced
- 450g (1lb) tomatoes, chopped
- 850ml (1½pints) vegetable stock (see recipe on page 20)
- 2tbsp chopped fresh basil
- sea salt and ground black pepper
- 2tbsp crème fraîche or light sour cream (optional)
- fresh basil sprigs, to garnish

serves *four*
preparation time *10 minutes*
cooking time *25–30 minutes*

method

1 Heat the oil in a large saucepan. Add the shallots, garlic and peppers, and cook for 5 minutes.
2 Add the tomatoes and stock. Cover, bring to the boil, then reduce the heat and simmer for 20–25 minutes, until the vegetables are tender.
3 Cool slightly, then purée in a blender or food processor until smooth. Press the mixture through a sieve and discard the pulp.
4 Return the soup to the rinsed-out saucepan, stir in the chopped basil and seasoning, and reheat gently until piping hot. Stir in the crème fraîche or light sour cream, if using.
5 Ladle into warmed soup bowls, garnish with the basil sprigs and serve with wholemeal rolls.

oven-baked turkey *with* mango salsa

To complement zinc-rich turkey, the mangoes in this tasty salsa provide carotenoids and vitamin C, which help with joint mobility.

ingredients

- 4 skinless, boneless turkey breast steaks
- 1tbsp olive oil
- 2tbsp wholegrain mustard
- 2tbsp chopped fresh tarragon
- sea salt
- freshly ground black pepper
- 1 onion, thinly sliced
- juice of 1 large lemon
- fresh herb sprigs, to garnish

for the salsa

- 1 large ripe mango, peeled, stoned and finely chopped
- 55g (2oz) cucumber, finely chopped
- 4 spring onions, finely chopped
- 1tbsp chopped fresh coriander

serves *four*
preparation time *15 minutes, plus 1–2 hours standing time*
cooking time *30–45 minutes*

method

1 First make the salsa. Put the mango, cucumber, spring onions and coriander in a bowl and mix well. Cover and leave to stand at room temperature for 1–2 hours.

2 Preheat the oven to 190°C/375°F/gas mark 5.

3 Cut four pieces of greaseproof paper, each large enough to wrap a steak. Cut three slashes in each steak and place on the paper.

4 Mix together the oil, mustard, tarragon and seasoning in a small bowl. Spread some of the mixture over each steak.

5 Add a few slices of onion, then drizzle lemon juice over the top. Fold the paper over the steaks and twist the edges to secure, making four parcels.

6 Place on a baking tray and bake for 30–45 minutes, until the turkey is cooked and tender.

7 Unwrap the parcels carefully (to avoid getting burnt by steam) and place the turkey on warmed serving plates. Spoon the juices on top and the salsa alongside. Garnish with the herb sprigs.

8 Serve with sautéed potatoes and grilled peppers (capsicums).

marbled cheesecake

This delicious fruity cheesecake is a real treat. Blackcurrants are an excellent source of potassium and vitamin C.

ingredients

- 175g (6oz) frozen blackcurrants, cherries or raspberries, defrosted
- 100g (3½oz) light brown sugar
- 85g (3oz) butter, chopped
- 175g (6oz) oat biscuits, crushed
- 1tbsp powdered gelatine
- 115g (4oz) curd (cottage) cheese
- 115g (4oz) plain yoghurt
- 150ml (¼ pint) single (pouring) cream
- finely grated rind and juice of 1 lemon
- 2 medium eggs, separated
- small bunches of redcurrants and fresh mint sprigs, to decorate

serves *six to eight*
preparation time *25 minutes, plus chilling time*

method

1 Purée the fruit and 40g (1½oz) sugar in a food processor. Press through a sieve. Set aside.

2 Melt the butter in a saucepan. Remove from the heat and stir in the biscuit crumbs. Press the mixture over the base of a 20cm (8in), loose-bottomed, deep cake tin. Chill for 30 minutes.

3 Sprinkle the gelatine over 3tbsp water in a small bowl. Soak for a couple of minutes, then place over a pan of simmering water and stir until dissolved.

4 Place the remaining sugar, curd cheese, yoghurt, cream, lemon rind and juice, and egg yolks in a food processor and blend. Add the gelatine and blend until well mixed. Pour into a bowl.

5 Whisk the egg whites until stiff, then fold into the cheese mixture. Pour over the biscuit base.

6 Pour the fruit purée in a thin stream over the cheese mixture and swirl to create a marbled effect. Refrigerate until set.

7 Remove from the tin and decorate with the redcurrants and mint sprigs.

warning

To reduce the risk of salmonella, buy only very fresh eggs in unbroken shells, refrigerate them immediately, and use them as quickly as possible. It is best to avoid uncooked eggs altogether if serving children, elderly people, or anyone with a compromised immune system.

beauty

In this section, we suggest numerous foods to feed your skin, nails, hair and eyes, and have devised some fabulous recipes to help detoxify your system and reshape your body. By eating lightly for a couple of days, and by drinking plenty of water, you give your liver and digestive system a rest, which in turn encourages the elimination of toxins that 'sit' on your hips and thighs. All fresh fruits and vegetables are packed with vitamins and fibre to aid the elimination process and are excellent detoxifiers. To reduce fatty deposits and cellulite on the hips and thighs, avoid saturated fats, sugar, coffee, alcohol and full-fat dairy produce, and make sure you get some exercise.

For glowing, healthy skin, eat plenty of carrots, tomatoes, orange-fleshed melons, spinach, red sweet potatoes and apricots, which are good sources of beta carotene, the plant form of vitamin A. Oily fish, walnuts, linseeds, sunflower and pumpkin seeds, and the unrefined oils of these nuts and seeds, are rich in

FOODS

essential fatty acids and vitamin E. For healthy skin, hair and nails you also need vitamins A and B, and the minerals silica, iron and zinc. Ensure you get enough of these by making brown rice, oats, sardines, wheatgerm, Brewer's yeast, pumpkin seeds, raisins, broccoli, peas and sweet potatoes a regular part of your diet. If you have longitudinal ridges in your nails, this may be a sign that you are not absorbing sufficient nutrients from your food. In this case, eat a little pineapple, papaya or pawpaw, or take a digestive enzyme tablet (available from health food shops), with meals.

For healthy eyes, eat lamb's liver (for vitamins A and B), oily fish (for vitamin B_{12} and essential fatty acids), and carrots, spinach, broccoli and apricots (for vitamin A derived from beta carotene). All berry fruits, including bilberries, blueberries and blackberries, contain flavonoids, which help to strengthen the small capillaries, reduce the tendency to night blindness and lower the risk of cataracts.

fresh *start*

A WELL-BALANCED DIET *is vital for optimal health, so if you eat sensibly most of the time, there should be no need to fast or restrict your diet. But if you have over-indulged, perhaps on holiday, you may benefit from following a detoxification regime for a day or two, to help cleanse the system. On detox days, ignore normal mealtimes and eat when you feel hungry. Good foods to include are fresh fruit and vegetables, yoghurt and brown rice. Avoid fatty meat, sugary foods, salty snacks, alcohol and caffeine. Drink plenty of water, low-fat milk and unsweetened fruit juices, relax as much as possible and take some gentle exercise.*

mango *and* apricot smoothie

This naturally sweet fruit drink is excellent as part of a cleansing programme. Mangoes and apricots are rich in vitamin C and other antioxidants.

ingredients

- 1 large ripe mango
- 8 ripe apricots

serves *two*
(makes approx 425ml/¾ pint)
preparation time *10 minutes*

method

1 Peel and stone the mango, and roughly chop the flesh. Halve and stone the apricots.

2 Place the mango flesh and apricots in a blender or food processor with 200ml (7fl oz) water and blend until smooth.

3 Press the mixture through a sieve and discard the pulp.

4 Pour the juice into glasses and serve immediately, or cover and chill before serving.

variations

- *Use 1 small pineapple instead of the mango.*
- *Use freshly squeezed orange juice instead of water.*

banana yoghurt shake

This creamy banana yoghurt shake can be whizzed up in no time at all. Bananas are packed full of nutrients, including potassium, magnesium, vitamin B_6 and vitamin C.

ingredients

- 300ml (½ pint) plain yoghurt
- 2 bananas, peeled and sliced

serves *two*
(makes approx 500ml/18fl oz)
preparation time *5 minutes*

method

1. Put the yoghurt and bananas in a blender or food processor and blend until smooth.
2. Pour into glasses and serve immediately.

variation

- *Use other fruits, such as 225g (8oz) strawberries or peaches, instead of bananas.*

citrus drink

This refreshing drink, with its sharp, fruity flavour, makes a great start to the day. Vitamin C is an antioxidant that is important in numerous body functions.

ingredients

- 1 pink (or standard) grapefruit
- 1 orange
- 2 kiwifruit
- 115g (4oz) strawberries

serves *two*
(makes approx 425ml/¾ pint)
preparation time *10 minutes*

method

1 Peel the grapefruit and orange, removing as much pith as possible, then break the fruit into segments. Peel and quarter the kiwifruit.

2 Place all the fruit in a blender or food processor and blend until smooth.

3 Press the mixture through a sieve and discard the pulp.

4 Pour the juice into glasses and serve immediately, or cover and chill before serving.

variations

- *Use raspberries instead of strawberries.*
- *Use 2 or 3 satsumas or clementines instead of the orange.*

chunky vegetable soup

Chunky vegetables cooked with herbs in home-made stock make a tasty, warming soup that is ideal for a cleansing programme. Carrots, turnips, potatoes and parsnips add antioxidants galore.

ingredients

- 1 large onion, finely chopped
- 2 sticks celery, chopped
- 225g (8oz) carrots, thinly sliced
- 225g (8oz) parsnips, diced
- 175g (6oz) potatoes or celeriac, diced
- 175g (6oz) turnip, diced
- 850ml (1½ pints) vegetable stock (see recipe on page 20)
- 2tsp dried *herbes de provence*
- sea salt
- freshly ground black pepper
- fresh herb sprigs, to garnish

serves *four*
preparation time *15 minutes*
cooking time *25 minutes*

method

1 Put all the vegetables in a saucepan with the stock, dried herbs and seasoning, and stir.

2 Cover, bring to the boil, then reduce the heat and simmer for about 25 minutes, until the vegetables are cooked and tender, stirring occasionally.

3 Ladle into warmed soup bowls and garnish with the herb sprigs.

variations

- *This soup can be puréed in a blender or food processor, if preferred. Reheat gently until piping hot.*
- *Use 2 leeks instead of the onion.*
- *Use swede and sweet potatoes instead of the turnip and parsnips.*

freezing instructions

Allow to cool completely, then transfer to a rigid, freezeproof container. Cover, seal and label. Freeze for up to 3 months. Defrost, and reheat gently in a saucepan until piping hot.

fresh pea *and* onion soup *with* parsley

A mixture of fresh vegetables makes a good soup for detox days. All culinary herbs are rich in nutrients and are a good way to add extra vitamins and minerals to dishes. Fresh parsley is more than a garnish – it's a good source of vitamin C.

ingredients

- 1tbsp olive oil
- 1 onion, finely chopped
- 2 leeks, washed and sliced
- 350g (12oz) potatoes, diced
- 225g (8oz) fresh shelled peas
- 850ml (1½ pints) vegetable stock (see recipe on page 20)
- sea salt
- freshly ground black pepper
- 2tbsp chopped fresh parsley
- fresh parsley sprigs, to garnish

serves *four to six*
preparation time *15 minutes*
cooking time *20–25 minutes*

method

1 Heat the oil in a large saucepan. Add the onion and leeks, and cook gently for 3 minutes, stirring.
2 Add the potatoes, peas, stock and seasoning, and stir to mix. Cover, bring to the boil, then reduce the heat and simmer for 15–20 minutes, stirring occasionally, until the vegetables are tender.
3 Remove the pan from the heat and set aside to cool slightly, then purée the soup in a blender or food processor until smooth.
4 Return the soup to the rinsed-out saucepan, add the chopped parsley and reheat gently until piping hot, stirring occasionally.
5 Ladle into soup bowls and garnish with the parsley sprigs.

variations

- *The soup does not have to be puréed, and the vegetables can be left in small pieces, if preferred.*
- *Use sweet potatoes instead of potatoes.*
- *Use chopped fresh tarragon instead of parsley.*

freezing instructions

Allow to cool completely, then transfer to a rigid, freezeproof container. Cover, seal and label. Freeze for up to 3 months. Defrost, and reheat gently in a saucepan until piping hot.

cucumber *and* mint soup

This soup makes a refreshing change on detox days. Garlic can lower cholesterol and blood pressure and also has anti-bacterial and anti-fungal properties. Yoghurt provides easily digestible protein, while cucumbers are low in calories.

ingredients

- 1 cucumber, seeded and diced
- 3 shallots (French shallots), chopped
- 1 large clove garlic, crushed
- 150ml (¼ pint) cold vegetable stock (see recipe on page 20)
- 300ml (½ pint) plain yoghurt
- 150ml (¼ pint) low-fat plain yoghurt
- 2–3tbsp chopped fresh mint
- sea salt
- freshly ground black pepper
- fresh mint sprigs, to garnish

serves *four*
preparation time *10 minutes, plus chilling time*

method

1 Put the cucumber, shallots, garlic and stock in a blender or food processor and blend until fairly smooth.

2 Add the yoghurt and blend until smooth. Pour the mixture into a bowl.

3 Stir in the chopped mint and season well with salt and pepper.

4 Cover and refrigerate for at least 1 hour before serving.

5 Ladle into soup bowls and serve garnished with the mint sprigs.

variations

- *Use chopped fresh tarragon or coriander instead of mint.*
- *Use 1 small onion instead of shallots.*

char-grilled vegetable salad

These grilled vegetables make a delicious starter or main dish and are excellent for detox days. Dandelion leaves give a vitamin boost to salads and are a natural diuretic.

ingredients

- 8 shallots (French shallots), thinly sliced
- 2 courgettes (zucchini), halved and then thinly sliced lengthways
- 2 red peppers (capsicums), seeded and sliced
- 1 small aubergine (eggplant), thinly sliced
- 4 plum (Roma) tomatoes, halved
- 115g (4oz) mixed dark-green salad leaves, such as spinach, young dandelion leaves and watercress
- 2tbsp chopped fresh parsley

for the dressing

- 3tbsp olive oil
- juice of 1 lemon
- sea salt
- freshly ground black pepper

serves *four to six*
preparation time *10 minutes*
cooking time *8–10 minutes*

method

1 Preheat the grill to high. Line the rack with foil. Put the shallots, courgettes, peppers, aubergine and tomatoes on the rack.

2 In a small bowl, whisk together the oil, lemon juice and seasoning. Lightly brush the vegetables with some of the oil mixture and grill for 8–10 minutes until cooked and tender. Halfway through the cooking time, turn the vegetables over and brush lightly with the oil mixture.

3 Divide the salad leaves between four or six serving plates. Spoon the vegetables on top and sprinkle with parsley.

4 Serve immediately, with a glass of freshly squeezed orange juice.

variations

- *Drizzle a little French dressing (see recipe on page 21) over the vegetables just before serving.*
- *Use standard red or yellow tomatoes instead of plum tomatoes.*
- *Use the juice of a lime instead of a lemon.*
- *Use chopped fresh mixed herbs or chives instead of parsley.*

exotic dried fruit compote

This simple compote of dried fruits and fruit juices is delicious and easy to make. It is a great recipe for a cleansing programme.

ingredients

- 350g (12oz) mixed exotic dried fruit, including mango, figs, pineapple, apricots and peaches
- 200ml (7fl oz) unsweetened apple or grape juice
- 200ml (7fl oz) unsweetened orange juice
- 1–2tsp ground mixed spice (optional)

serves *four*
preparation time *5 minutes, plus 4 hours standing time*

method

1 Put the dried fruit in a serving bowl. Add the apple or grape juice, orange juice and mixed spice, if using. Stir to mix well.
2 Cover and chill in the refrigerator overnight.
3 Serve with plain yoghurt.

variations

- *Serve the fruit salad warm. After leaving it to stand overnight in the refrigerator, put the fruit and juices in a saucepan and bring gently to the boil. Remove the pan from the heat and set aside to cool slightly before serving.*
- *Chop the fruit before soaking in the fruit juices.*

five fruit salad

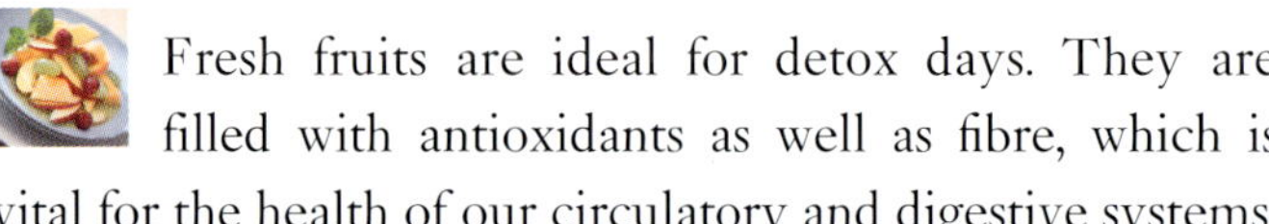

Fresh fruits are ideal for detox days. They are filled with antioxidants as well as fibre, which is vital for the health of our circulatory and digestive systems.

ingredients

- 300ml (½ pint) unsweetened grape juice
- 300ml (½ pint) unsweetened orange juice
- 1 small melon
- 2 ripe peaches
- 2 eating apples
- 115g (4oz) green seedless grapes
- 175g (6oz) fresh raspberries
- fresh mint sprigs, to decorate

serves *six*
preparation time *15 minutes, plus 2–3 hours standing time*

method

1 Put the grape and orange juices in a serving bowl and stir.
2 Halve, peel and seed the melon and dice the flesh. Peel and stone the peaches and chop the flesh. Add the melon and peaches to the fruit juices.
3 Peel, core and slice or chop the apples and add to the fruit juices with the grapes and raspberries. Stir gently.
4 Cover and refrigerate for 2–3 hours before serving, to allow the flavours to blend.
5 Decorate with the mint sprigs and serve with plain yoghurt.

variations

- *Use a small pineapple instead of the melon.*
- *Use nectarines instead of peaches.*
- *Use pears and strawberries instead of apples and raspberries.*

shape *foods*

A HEALTHY DIET *includes plenty of vegetables, fruit and complex carbohydrates, or starches (bread, cereals, potatoes, pulses and pasta) and moderate amounts of protein-rich, low-fat dairy foods, eggs, chicken, fish and lean meat. By eating a variety of foods in sensible proportions, you can obtain all the nutrients you need.*

Italian chicken casserole

Chicken portions are braised with vegetables to make this succulent dish. Cooked without the skin, chicken is an excellent protein food, low in saturated fat.

ingredients

- 1tbsp olive oil
- 4 skinless chicken portions
- 350g (12oz) baby (pickling) onions
- 1 clove garlic, crushed
- 1 red pepper (capsicum), seeded and diced
- 225g (8oz) button mushrooms
- 400g (14oz) can tomatoes, chopped
- 150ml (¼ pint) chicken stock (see recipe on page 20)
- 150ml (¼ pint) red wine
- 1tbsp chopped fresh thyme
- 1tbsp chopped fresh oregano
- sea salt
- freshly ground black pepper
- fresh herb sprigs, to garnish

serves *four*
preparation time *15 minutes*
cooking time *1 hour*

method

1 Preheat the oven to 180°C/350°F/gas mark 4.

2 Heat the oil in a flameproof, ovenproof casserole dish. Add the chicken and cook until sealed all over, turning occasionally.

3 Add all the remaining ingredients, except the herb garnish, and stir. Bring to the boil, stirring occasionally.

4 Cover and bake for about 1 hour, until the chicken and vegetables are cooked and tender, stirring once or twice.

5 Using a slotted spoon, place the chicken and vegetables on warmed plates and keep hot.

6 Bring the sauce to the boil and boil rapidly for a few minutes, until it has reduced and thickened. Spoon the sauce over the chicken and vegetables.

7 Garnish with the herb sprigs.

8 Serve with cooked fresh vegetables, such as broccoli and cauliflower florets.

variations

- *Use small turkey portions instead of chicken.*
- *Use shallots (French shallots) instead of baby onions.*
- *Use white wine or unsweetened apple juice instead of red wine.*

freezing instructions

Allow to cool completely, then transfer to a rigid, freezeproof container. Cover, seal and label. Freeze for up to 3 months. Defrost completely, and reheat in a moderate oven until piping hot.

fish provençale

These oven-baked fish fillets are served with a generous portion of delicious vegetable sauce. Fresh fish is a protein food and is rich in selenium, magnesium and omega-3 fatty acids.

ingredients

- 1 onion, sliced
- 1 clove garlic, crushed
- 1 red pepper (capsicum), seeded and sliced
- 1 yellow pepper (capsicum), seeded and sliced
- 2 courgettes (zucchini), sliced
- 400g (14oz) can tomatoes, chopped
- sea salt
- freshly ground black pepper
- 4 fish fillets, such as haddock or gemfish, each weighing about 175g (6oz)
- juice of 1 large lemon
- 2tbsp chopped fresh parsley
- 2tbsp chopped fresh basil
- 55g (2oz) black olives
- fresh herb sprigs, to garnish

serves *four*
preparation time *10 minutes*
cooking time *20 minutes*

method

1 Preheat the oven to 180°C/350°F/gas mark 4.

2 Put the onion, garlic, peppers, courgettes, tomatoes and seasoning in a saucepan and stir. Cover, bring to the boil, then reduce the heat and simmer for about 20 minutes, until the vegetables are tender, stirring occasionally.

3 Meanwhile, place the fish fillets in a shallow ovenproof dish. Drizzle with lemon juice and sprinkle with parsley. Cover and bake for 15–20 minutes, until the flesh just flakes when tested with a fork.

4 Stir the basil into the sauce.

5 Put the fillets on warmed serving plates, spoon some sauce over and scatter the olives on top. Garnish with the herb sprigs.

6 Serve hot with cooked fresh vegetables, such as green beans and baby sweetcorn.

variations

- *Use the juice of 2 limes instead of a lemon.*
- *Use 1 aubergine (eggplant) instead of courgettes.*

grilled lamb cutlets *with* plum tomato salsa

Lamb cutlets grilled and served with a tomato salsa make an appetising dish. Tomatoes are particularly rich in vitamin C, lycopene and other carotenoids, as well as dietary fibre. These nutrients are believed to help protect the body against cancer.

ingredients

- 700g (1lb 9oz) plum (Roma) tomatoes, skinned, seeded and finely chopped
- 2 spring onions, chopped
- 1 large clove garlic, crushed
- 1tbsp olive oil
- 1tbsp sun-dried tomato purée (paste)
- 1–2tsp balsamic vinegar
- 2tbsp chopped fresh basil
- sea salt
- freshly ground black pepper
- 8 lean lamb cutlets

serves *four*
preparation time *15 minutes, plus 1 hour standing time*
cooking time *8–12 minutes*

method

1 Put the tomatoes, spring onions, garlic, oil, tomato purée, vinegar, basil and seasoning in a bowl and mix well. Cover and leave at room temperature for about 1 hour, to allow the flavours to blend.

2 Preheat the grill to high. Place the cutlets on a rack in a grill pan. Grill for 4–6 minutes on each side, until cooked.

3 Place the cutlets on serving plates, with the tomato salsa spooned alongside.

4 Serve with cooked fresh vegetables, such as spinach, peas and baby (Dutch) carrots.

variations

- *Use 2 shallots (French shallots) instead of spring onions.*
- *Use chopped fresh chives or coriander instead of basil.*
- *Serve the tomato salsa with other grilled lean meats, such as chicken or turkey breasts.*

tuna steaks baked *with* spices

These fresh tuna steaks baked with spices and lemon are delicious served with fresh seasonal vegetables. Tuna is an excellent protein food, and a good source of omega-3 fatty acids.

ingredients

- 4 tuna steaks, each weighing about 175g (6oz)
- 2tsp coriander seeds
- 2tsp cumin seeds
- 1tsp dried, crushed chillies
- 1tsp black peppercorns
- sea salt
- finely grated rind and juice of 1 large lemon

serves *four*
preparation time *10 minutes*
cooking time *20 minutes*

method

1 Preheat the oven to 190°C/375°F/gas mark 5.
2 Cut four pieces of non-stick baking paper, each large enough to wrap a tuna steak. Place a steak on each.
3 Put the seeds, crushed chillies, peppercorns and salt in a mortar. Using a pestle, crush the spices to break them up a little. Stir in the lemon rind.
4 Scatter the spice mixture evenly over the fish steaks, then drizzle with a little lemon juice. Fold the paper over the fish and twist the edges to secure, making four parcels.
5 Transfer the parcels to a baking tray and bake for about 20 minutes, until the flesh just flakes when tested with a fork. (When unwrapping to test, beware of steam.)
6 Place the unopened parcels on warmed serving plates and serve immediately with cooked fresh vegetables, such as baby sweetcorn and carrots.

variations

- *Use salmon steaks instead of tuna.*
- *Use 1 large lime or 1 small orange instead of a lemon.*
- *Use mixed peppercorns instead of black peppercorns.*

peppers stuffed *with* herbed rice

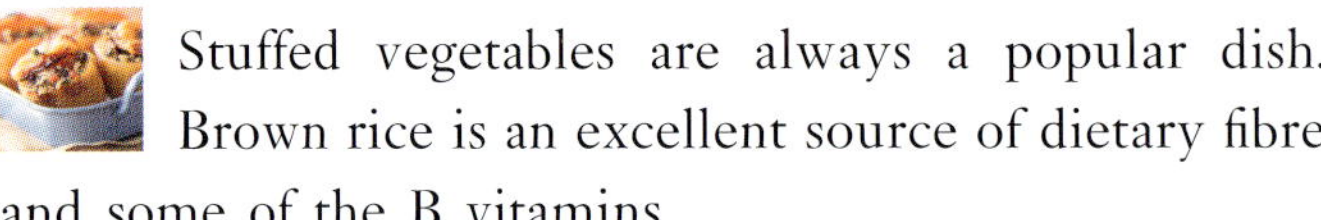

Stuffed vegetables are always a popular dish. Brown rice is an excellent source of dietary fibre and some of the B vitamins.

ingredients

- 4 large peppers (capsicums)
- 1tbsp olive oil
- 4 shallots (French shallots), finely chopped
- 1 clove garlic, crushed
- 115g (4oz) mushrooms, finely chopped
- 1 courgette (zucchini), finely chopped
- 175g (6oz) cooked brown rice
- 2 tomatoes, skinned, seeded and finely chopped
- 55g (2oz) pine nuts, finely chopped
- 55g (2oz) pitted black olives, finely chopped
- 2tbsp chopped fresh mixed herbs
- sea salt
- freshly ground black pepper

serves *four*
preparation time *25 minutes*
cooking time *35–40 minutes*

method

1 Preheat the oven to 180°C/350°F/gas mark 4.

2 Slice the tops off the peppers and remove and discard the cores and seeds. Cook in boiling water for 4 minutes, then drain.

3 Heat the oil in a saucepan, add the shallots, garlic, mushrooms and courgettes, and cook for 5 minutes, stirring occasionally. Remove from the heat and add all the remaining ingredients.

4 Spoon some stuffing into each pepper and top with the lids. Place in a shallow ovenproof dish and add a little water. Cover with foil and bake for 35–40 minutes, until tender.

5 Serve with a mixed leaf salad.

variations

- *Use almonds or hazelnuts instead of pine nuts.*
- *Use 1 leek instead of the shallots.*
- *Use couscous instead of rice.*

potato, leek *and* coriander rösti

These potato rösti are sure to be popular with the whole family. Potatoes are rich in dietary fibre, potassium and vitamin C.

ingredients

- 700g (1lb 9oz) potatoes, washed and left whole and unpeeled
- 2tbsp olive oil
- 2 leeks, washed and thinly sliced
- 2–3tbsp chopped fresh coriander
- sea salt
- freshly ground black pepper

serves *four to six*
preparation time *15 minutes, plus cooling time*
cooking time *20–25 minutes*

method

1 Preheat the oven to 220°C/425°F/gas mark 7.
2 Grease two baking trays.
3 Parboil the potatoes in a saucepan of boiling water for 6 minutes. Drain and set aside to cool slightly.
4 When cool enough to handle, peel the potatoes and coarsely grate them into a bowl. Set aside.
5 Heat the oil in a large non-stick frying pan. Add the leeks and cook for about 5 minutes, until softened, stirring occasionally. Remove the pan from the heat.
6 Add the leeks, coriander and seasoning to the potatoes and stir. Spoon 12 small mounds of the mixture onto the baking trays.
7 Bake for 20–25 minutes, until golden brown and crisp.
8 Serve immediately, with cooked fresh vegetables, such as spinach and grilled tomatoes.

variations

- *Use 2 onions instead of the leeks.*
- *Use chopped fresh parsley, basil or tarragon instead of coriander.*

tomato *and* broad bean couscous salad

Couscous makes a good grain base for a salad. Tossed with vegetables and a light, flavourful dressing, it makes an excellent light meal. Tomatoes and peppers (capsicums) are rich sources of vitamin C; tomatoes are also a good source of the potentially anti-cancer compound lycopene.

ingredients

- 225g (8oz) quick-cook (instant) couscous
- 225g (8oz) fresh or frozen broad beans
- 350g (12oz) cherry tomatoes, halved
- 1 yellow pepper (capsicum), seeded and diced
- 6–8 spring onions, chopped
- half a cucumber, diced

for the dressing

- 150ml (¼ pint) tomato juice
- 1 clove garlic, crushed
- 2tsp balsamic vinegar
- ½tsp brown sugar
- 2tbsp chopped fresh coriander
- sea salt
- freshly ground black pepper

serves *four to six*
preparation time *15 minutes, plus cooling and standing time*
cooking time *10–15 minutes*

method

1 Cook the couscous according to the directions. Set aside to cool, then place in a large serving bowl.

2 Cook the broad beans in a saucepan of boiling water for 6–8 minutes, until cooked and tender. Drain well, then rinse under cold running water to cool quickly, and drain again.

3 Stir the broad beans, tomatoes, yellow pepper, spring onions and cucumber into the couscous.

4 Place the dressing ingredients in a small bowl and whisk together. Pour over the couscous salad and toss the ingredients together.

5 Cover and leave at room temperature for 1 hour before serving, or cover and chill for several hours before serving, to allow the flavours to blend.

6 Serve with a mixed pepper and onion salad.

variations

- *Use pasta instead of couscous.*
- *Use standard or plum (Roma) tomatoes instead of cherry tomatoes.*
- *Use peas or green beans instead of broad beans.*

roast vegetables *with* garlic *and* fresh herbs

This is a simple but delicious way of serving mixed vegetables. The artichokes add flavour and texture as well as plentiful supplies of beta carotene, folate and potassium.

ingredients

- 2 onions, each cut into 8 pieces
- 4 courgettes (zucchini), cut into chunks
- 1 red pepper (capsicum), seeded and cut into large chunks
- 1 yellow pepper (capsicum), seeded and cut into large chunks
- 225g (8oz) button mushrooms
- 175g (6oz) baby sweetcorn
- 2 cloves garlic, finely chopped
- 2tbsp olive oil
- 4 tomatoes, halved
- 400g (14oz) can artichoke hearts, rinsed, drained and halved
- 2–3tbsp chopped fresh mixed herbs
- sea salt
- freshly ground black pepper

serves *four to six*
preparation time *15 minutes*
cooking time *30–35 minutes*

method

1 Preheat the oven to 220°C/425°F/gas mark 7.

2 Put the onions, courgettes, peppers, mushrooms, sweetcorn and garlic in a large roasting tin and stir to mix. Add the oil and toss the vegetables to coat them lightly all over.

3 Bake for 20 minutes, stirring once.

4 Add the tomatoes and artichoke hearts, and stir. Bake for a further 10–15 minutes, until the vegetables are just cooked and tinged brown at the edges.

5 Sprinkle with the herbs and seasoning. Stir and serve with a mixed leaf salad.

variations

- *Use a mixture of baby vegetables.*
- *Use 250g (9oz) cherry tomatoes instead of standard tomatoes.*
- *Use sesame oil instead of olive oil.*

vegetable based

carrot, courgette *and* broccoli stir-fry

This stir-fry of vegetables makes a great light meal or snack. Carrots and broccoli are excellent sources of carotenoids.

ingredients

- 2tbsp olive oil
- 2 carrots, cut into matchstick (julienne) strips
- 2 courgettes (zucchini), cut into matchstick (julienne) strips
- 225g (8oz) small broccoli florets, halved
- 1 large clove garlic, finely chopped
- 2.5cm (1in) piece of fresh root ginger, peeled and finely chopped or grated
- 115g (4oz) beansprouts
- 1tbsp fresh lemon juice
- 1tbsp light soy sauce
- sea salt
- freshly ground black pepper

serves *four*
preparation time *15 minutes*
cooking time *5–7 minutes*

method

1 Heat the oil in a non-stick wok or large frying pan. Add the carrots, courgettes, broccoli, garlic and ginger, and stir-fry over a high heat for 4–5 minutes.

2 Add the beansprouts, lemon juice and soy sauce, and stir-fry for a further 1–2 minutes, until the vegetables are just cooked.

3 Season to taste with salt and pepper, and serve with grilled tomatoes and peppers.

variations

- *Use cauliflower florets or sliced mushrooms instead of broccoli florets.*
- *Use 115g (4oz) shredded spinach instead of courgettes.*
- *Use dry sherry instead of lemon juice.*
- *Use sesame oil instead of olive oil.*

oven-baked vegetable compote

This vegetable compote provides a range of nutrients, including beta carotene (for vitamin A), vitamin C, selenium and zinc.

ingredients

- 400g (14oz) can tomatoes, chopped
- 2tsp dried *herbes de provence*
- sea salt
- freshly ground black pepper
- 1 onion, thinly sliced
- 2 leeks, washed and thinly sliced
- 4 sticks celery, chopped
- 1 red pepper (capsicum), seeded and sliced
- 1 yellow pepper (capsicum), seeded and sliced
- 1 small aubergine (eggplant), thickly sliced
- 2 courgettes (zucchini), sliced
- 2 carrots, thinly sliced
- 115g (4oz) button mushrooms
- fresh herb sprigs, to garnish

serves *four to six*
preparation time *15 minutes*
cooking time *1 hour*

method

1 Preheat the oven to 190°C/375°F/gas mark 5.

2 Put the tomatoes, dried herbs and seasoning in a large ovenproof casserole dish and stir. Add all the remaining ingredients, except the herb garnish, and stir.

3 Cover and bake for 1 hour, until the vegetables are cooked and tender, stirring once or twice.

4 Garnish with the herb sprigs and serve hot on its own or with a mixed salad.

variations

- *Use 6 shallots (French shallots) instead of the onion.*
- *Use 175g (6oz) diced swede or turnip instead of carrots.*
- *Use baby sweetcorn instead of button mushrooms.*

freezing instructions

Allow to cool completely, then transfer to a rigid, freezeproof container. Cover, seal and label. Freeze for up to 3 months. Defrost, and reheat gently in a moderate oven until hot.

vegetable curry

This mild vegetable curry makes a filling evening meal. Vegetables are excellent nutritional all-rounders, because they contain beta carotene (for vitamin A), vitamin C, potassium and fibre. Extra virgin olive oil is a monounsaturated fat.

ingredients

- 1tbsp olive oil
- 1 large onion, sliced
- 2 cloves garlic, finely chopped
- 1 small fresh red chilli, finely chopped
- 1 kg (2lb 4oz) mixed prepared fresh vegetables, including diced potatoes, swede, turnip, carrots and parsnips, plus small cauliflower florets and peas left whole
- 2tsp ground coriander
- 2tsp ground cumin
- 1½tsp ground turmeric
- 400g (14oz) can tomatoes, chopped
- 150ml (¼ pint) vegetable stock (see recipe on page 20)
- 150ml (¼ pint) coconut milk
- sea salt
- freshly ground black pepper
- 1tbsp cornflour
- 2tbsp chopped fresh coriander, to garnish

serves *four to six*
preparation time *15 minutes*
cooking time *35–50 minutes*

method

1 Heat the oil in a saucepan. Add the onion, garlic and chilli, and cook for 5 minutes.

2 Stir in all the remaining ingredients, except the cornflour and coriander garnish. Cover, bring to the boil, then reduce the heat and simmer for 30–45 minutes, until the vegetables are cooked, stirring occasionally.

3 Blend the cornflour with 4tbsp water and stir into the curry. Bring to the boil, stirring continuously, then simmer for 2 minutes.

4 Serve the curry on a bed of couscous or brown rice, and garnish with the coriander.

variations

- *Use 3–4tsp curry powder instead of the fresh chilli and ground spices.*
- *Use 8 shallots (French shallots) instead of the onion.*
- *Use additional stock instead of coconut milk.*
- *If you prefer a hot curry, add more ground spices to taste.*

freezing instructions

Allow to cool completely, then transfer to a rigid, freezeproof container. Cover, seal and label. Freeze for up to 3 months. Defrost, and reheat gently in a saucepan until hot.

skin *and* nail foods

*F*OR HEALTHY SKIN *and nails, the body needs sufficient amounts of all the vitamins, as well as calcium, iron, selenium and zinc. The vitamin B group is important for the repair and regeneration of skin tissue – signs of deficiency include cracks and sores around the mouth and nose.*

Vitamin C is needed for the production of collagen and is vital for wound healing and resistance to infection. Common signs of vitamin C deficiency are bleeding gums, cuts that won't heal and broken capillaries. Pale, concave nails and itchy skin may indicate iron deficiency.

watercress soup

Serve this delicious, warming soup with wholemeal bread. Watercress is a great skin food, rich in carotenoids and vitamin C.

ingredients

- 1tbsp olive oil
- 1 onion, chopped
- 225g (8oz) potatoes, diced
- 3 sticks celery, finely chopped
- 225g (8oz) watercress, roughly chopped
- 600ml (1 pint) vegetable stock (see recipe on page 20)
- 300ml (½ pint) milk
- sea salt
- freshly ground black pepper
- small watercress sprigs, to garnish

serves *four*
preparation time *15 minutes*
cooking time *20–25 minutes*

method

1 Heat the oil in a large saucepan. Add the onion, potatoes and celery. Cook gently for 5 minutes, stirring occasionally.
2 Add the watercress, stock, milk and seasoning, and mix well. Cover, bring to the boil, then reduce the heat and simmer for 15–20 minutes, stirring occasionally, until the vegetables are cooked and tender.
3 Remove the pan from the heat, cool slightly, then purée the soup in a blender or food processor until smooth.
4 Return the soup to the rinsed-out saucepan and reheat gently until hot, stirring occasionally.
5 To serve, ladle into warmed soup bowls and garnish with the watercress sprigs.
6 Serve with wholemeal bread or rolls.

variations

- *For a delicious broccoli soup, replace the watercress with 350g (12oz) broccoli florets.*
- *Use sweet potatoes instead of standard potatoes.*
- *Use 6 shallots (French shallots) or 1 leek instead of the onion.*

shredded beetroot *and* carrot salad

This salad of shredded root vegetables and dark-green salad leaves is tossed in a honey-lemon dressing. Beetroot is an excellent source of folate, vitamin C, magnesium and potassium.

ingredients

- 350g (12oz) carrots
- 225g (8oz) raw beetroot
- 115g (4oz) mixed dark-green salad leaves, such as spinach, watercress, lollo rosso (coral lettuce), red (ruby) chard and rocket
- 2tbsp chopped fresh mixed herbs
- 25–55g (1–2oz) toasted hazelnuts, roughly chopped

for the dressing

- 2tbsp hazelnut oil
- 1tbsp olive oil
- juice of 1 lemon
- 1tbsp honey
- 1 clove garlic, crushed
- sea salt
- freshly ground black pepper

serves *four*
preparation time *15 minutes*

method

1 Peel and coarsely grate or shred the carrots and beetroot. Put in a bowl.

2 Add the salad leaves and mixed herbs, and toss. Divide the salad between four serving plates.

3 Put the oils, lemon juice, honey, garlic and seasoning in a bowl and whisk until well mixed.

4 Drizzle the dressing over the salads and toss to mix.

5 Scatter with chopped hazelnuts, and serve immediately, with crusty wholemeal bread.

variations

- *Use lime juice instead of lemon.*
- *Use courgettes (zucchini) instead of beetroot.*
- *Use almonds or pecan nuts instead of hazelnuts.*

grilled sardines *with* cucumber relish

This quick and easy recipe combines fresh sardines with a tasty cucumber relish. Oily fish such as sardines are a good source of vitamins A and D, B vitamins, selenium and omega-3 fatty acids, all of which are good skin and nail nutrients.

ingredients

- 900g (2lb) large sardines, gutted and cleaned if preferred
- 2tbsp olive oil
- juice of 1 lime
- 1tsp dried mixed herbs

for the relish

- half a cucumber, finely chopped
- 2 shallots (French shallots), finely chopped
- 1 clove garlic, crushed
- 150g (5½oz) plain yoghurt
- 1–2tbsp chopped fresh mint
- sea salt
- freshly ground black pepper

serves *four to six*
preparation time *15 minutes*
cooking time *8–14 minutes*

method

1 Put the cucumber, shallots, garlic, yoghurt, mint and seasoning in a bowl and mix well. Cover and set aside.

2 Preheat the grill to high. Cover a grill rack with foil and place the sardines on the rack.

3 Put the oil, lime juice, dried herbs and seasoning in a bowl and mix well. Brush the sardines lightly all over with the oil mixture.

4 Grill the sardines for about 4–7 minutes on each side, until cooked.

5 Place the sardines on serving dishes with the cucumber relish spooned alongside.

6 Serve with baked potatoes and a crisp green salad.

variations

- *Use small mackerel or other small oily fish instead of sardines.*
- *Use fresh basil instead of mint.*
- *Use lemon or orange juice instead of lime juice.*
- *Use 4 spring onions instead of the shallots.*

chinese-style roast lemon chicken

Serve this delicious lemon chicken with crisp roast potatoes and fresh vegetables for an appetising meal. Poultry is a good source of protein and B vitamins, nutrients for skin and hair health.

ingredients

- 1tbsp light soy sauce
- 1tbsp dry sherry
- rind and juice of 1 lemon
- 2 shallots (French shallots), chopped
- 5cm (2in) piece of fresh root ginger, peeled and chopped
- 2tbsp chopped fresh coriander
- sea salt
- freshly ground black pepper
- 1.5 kg (3lb 5oz) whole chicken
- 1 lemon, thickly sliced
- 25g (1oz) butter, melted
- 300ml (½ pint) chicken stock (see recipe on page 20)

serves *four*
preparation time *15 minutes*
cooking time *1½ hours*

method

1 Preheat the oven to 200°C/400°F/gas mark 6.

2 Put the soy sauce, sherry, lemon rind and juice, shallots, ginger, coriander and seasoning in a blender or food processor and blend until fairly smooth and well mixed.

3 Lift the skin flap on the chicken and loosen the skin over the breast, trying to avoid breaking the skin. Insert the puréed mixture under the skin and spread it out in an even layer.

4 Put the lemon slices in the chicken cavity.

5 Weigh the bird and calculate the cooking time, allowing 20 minutes per 450g (1lb), plus 20 minutes.

6 Place the chicken in a roasting tin and brush all over with the melted butter. Pour the stock around the base of the chicken.

7 Roast, uncovered, for about 1½ hours, until the chicken is cooked and tender and the juices run clear. Cover the chicken with foil once it is well browned.

8 Carve the chicken and serve with roast potatoes, braised carrots and celery.

variations

- *For poached lemon chicken, follow the recipe above, but don't brush the chicken with butter. Put the chicken in a large saucepan and cover with water. Cover, bring to the boil and poach gently for 50–60 minutes, until the chicken is cooked and tender. Carve and serve. The poaching liquid can be boiled rapidly until reduced to make a tasty sauce.*
- *Use 1 lime instead of the lemon.*
- *Use chopped fresh tarragon instead of coriander.*

turkey *and* brussels sprouts stir-fry

Sunflower seeds add flavour and texture to this quick and easy stir-fry. They are an especially good source of vitamin E, making them a great skin food.

ingredients

- 1tbsp sesame oil
- 350g (12oz) skinless, boneless turkey breast, cut into thin strips
- 1 clove garlic, crushed
- 225g (8oz) Brussels sprouts, shredded
- 1 red pepper (capsicum), seeded and sliced
- 6–8 spring onions, chopped
- 175g (6oz) mushrooms, sliced
- 2tbsp dry sherry
- 2tbsp light soy sauce
- freshly ground black pepper
- 1–2tbsp sunflower seeds

serves *four*
preparation time *15 minutes*
cooking time *8–10 minutes*

method

1 Heat the oil in a non-stick wok or large frying pan. Add the turkey and garlic, and stir-fry over a high heat for 2 minutes.

2 Add the Brussels sprouts and red pepper, and stir-fry for 2–3 minutes.

3 Add the spring onions and mushrooms, and stir-fry for a further 2–3 minutes.

4 Add the sherry, soy sauce and black pepper, and stir-fry until the mixture is piping hot and the turkey and vegetables are cooked and tender.

5 Scatter the turkey with sunflower seeds.

6 Serve with brown rice or rice noodles.

variations

- *Use chicken breast or lean lamb instead of turkey.*
- *Use courgettes (zucchini) or carrots instead of Brussels sprouts.*
- *Use unsweetened apple juice instead of sherry.*

roast sweet potatoes

Roast sweet potatoes make a great accompaniment to roast lean meat or fish. Red sweet potatoes are rich in beta carotene (which the body converts to vitamin A) and a good source of potassium and vitamin C, all excellent skin and nail foods.

ingredients

- 1 kg (2lb 4oz) red sweet potatoes
- 2–3tbsp olive oil
- 1 large clove garlic, finely chopped
- 1–2tbsp chopped fresh rosemary
- sea salt
- freshly ground black pepper

serves *four*
preparation time *15 minutes*
cooking time *45 minutes*

method

1 Preheat the oven to 220°C/425°F/gas mark 7.
2 Peel the potatoes, cut into chunks and put in a saucepan of cold, lightly salted water. Cover, bring to the boil and boil for 2 minutes. Drain well.
3 Heat the oil in a roasting tin in the oven for 3–4 minutes.
4 Add the potatoes, garlic, rosemary and seasoning, and turn the potatoes over in the oil mixture to coat.
5 Roast the potatoes for about 45 minutes, until golden brown and crisp, turning once or twice. Drain off any excess oil after about 35 minutes.
6 Serve with grilled meat or fish, and cooked vegetables, such as broccoli and cauliflower florets.

variations

- *Use parsnips or celeriac instead of sweet potatoes.*
- *Use fresh thyme or coriander instead of rosemary.*

fruit *and* nut rice salad

This delicious rice salad is excellent for a summertime picnic or buffet meal. Nuts such as Brazils and almonds are great skin foods, because they contain potassium, magnesium, selenium, iron and zinc.

ingredients

- 225g (8oz) long grain brown rice
- 1 yellow pepper (capsicum), seeded and diced
- 6–8 spring onions, chopped
- 2 red-skinned eating apples
- 175g (6oz) ready-to-eat dried apricots, chopped
- 115g (4oz) sultanas
- 115g (4oz) raisins
- 85g (3oz) Brazil nuts, roughly chopped
- 85g (3oz) almonds, roughly chopped

for the dressing

- 150ml (¼ pint) unsweetened orange juice
- 2tbsp olive oil
- 1tbsp wholegrain mustard
- 1tbsp balsamic vinegar
- 2tbsp chopped fresh parsley
- sea salt
- freshly ground black pepper

serves *six*
preparation time *15 minutes*
cooking time *30 minutes*

method

1 Cook the rice until tender. Rinse under cold running water and drain.

2 Put the rice in a serving bowl. Add the pepper, spring onions, apples, apricots, sultanas, raisins and nuts, and mix well.

3 Put all the dressing ingredients in a bowl and whisk together.

4 Pour the dressing over the rice salad and toss to mix well.

5 Serve with grilled lean meat or baked fish.

variations

- *Use ready-to-eat dried pears, peaches or figs instead of apricots.*
- *Use unsweetened apple or grape juice instead of orange juice.*
- *Use a mixture of brown and wild rice.*
- *Add a few pumpkin seeds for their essential fatty acids and iron.*

poached pears *with* blackcurrant sauce

Fresh pears poached with whole spices and served with a blackcurrant sauce make a mouth-watering dessert. Blackcurrants contain various antioxidants, including large amounts of vitamin C.

ingredients

- 300ml (½ pint) unsweetened apple juice or grape juice
- 85g (3oz) dark brown sugar
- 6 ripe pears, peeled and left whole with stalks intact
- pared rind of 1 lemon
- 1 cinnamon stick, broken in half
- 6 whole cloves
- 225g (8oz) fresh or frozen (defrosted) blackcurrants
- 2tsp arrowroot
- 2tbsp crème de cassis or blackcurrant liqueur
- fresh mint sprigs, to decorate

serves *six*
preparation time *10 minutes*
cooking time *40 minutes*

method

1 Put the apple or grape juice and sugar in a saucepan and heat gently until the sugar has dissolved, stirring continuously.
2 Add the pears, lemon rind, cinnamon stick and cloves, and stir. Cover, bring to the boil, then reduce the heat and simmer for about 15 minutes, until the pears are cooked and tender.
3 Using a slotted spoon, transfer the pears to a serving dish. Cover and keep them warm.
4 Remove and discard the lemon rind, cinnamon stick and cloves.
5 Add the blackcurrants to the pan, cover, bring to the boil, then reduce the heat and simmer for about 10 minutes, until soft, stirring occasionally.
6 Blend the arrowroot with the crème de cassis or liqueur and stir into the blackcurrant sauce. Heat gently, stirring continuously, until the sauce comes to the boil and thickens slightly.
7 Pour the sauce over the pears and decorate with the mint sprigs.
8 Serve warm or cold with plain yoghurt or home-made yoghurt ice.

variations

- *Use firm, ripe peaches or nectarines instead of pears.*
- *Use raspberries or blueberries instead of blackcurrants.*
- *Add an extra 1 teaspoon of arrowroot if you prefer a thicker sauce.*
- *Sprinkle with raw wheatgerm to add vitamin B.*

spicy grilled nectarines

This simple dessert is quick to make and delicious. Serve it with plain yoghurt, crème fraîche or light sour cream. Nectarines are good skin foods because they contain plenty of vitamin C.

ingredients

- 4 large ripe nectarines
- 2tbsp unsweetened orange juice
- 2tbsp honey
- 1–2tsp ground mixed spice

serves *two to four*
preparation time *10 minutes*
cooking time *4–5 minutes*

method

1 Put the nectarines in a large saucepan of boiling water for 15 seconds. Remove with a slotted spoon and plunge into a bowl of cold water. Drain, then peel off the skins, using a sharp knife.

2 Preheat the grill to high. Cover a grill rack with foil. Cut each nectarine in half, remove the stone, then cut the fruit into quarters or slices. Place on the grill rack.

3 Put the orange juice, honey and spice in a bowl and stir. Drizzle over the nectarines.

4 Grill the nectarines for about 4–5 minutes, until hot, turning once or twice. Serve with plain yoghurt, crème fraîche or light sour cream.

variations

- *Use peaches instead of nectarines.*
- *Use ground ginger or cinnamon instead of mixed spice.*
- *Use maple syrup instead of honey.*

banana *and* date tealoaf

Serve this delicately spiced banana and date tealoaf in slices on its own or spread with a little butter or honey. Bananas contain a number of skin- and nail-boosting nutrients.

ingredients

- 225g (8oz) plain wholemeal flour
- 2tsp baking powder
- 1tsp ground mixed spice or nutmeg
- 115g (4oz) butter, chopped
- 115g (4oz) light brown sugar
- 115g (4oz) thick honey
- 2 medium eggs, beaten
- 2 large bananas, peeled and mashed with a little lemon juice
- 115g (4oz) dried dates, finely chopped

serves *eight to ten.*
preparation time *20 minutes*
cooking time *1–1¼ hours*

method

1 Preheat the oven to 180°C/350°F/gas mark 4. Grease and line a 900g (2lb) loaf tin.

2 Put the flour, baking powder and spice in a bowl. Lightly rub in the butter until the mixture resembles breadcrumbs.

3 Add the sugar, honey, eggs, bananas and dates, and beat until well mixed. Turn the mixture into the loaf tin.

4 Bake for 1–1¼ hours, until well risen and firm to the touch.

5 Cool slightly in the tin, then turn out onto a wire rack to cool.

6 Serve plain or spread with a little butter, preserve or honey.

variations

- *Brush the top of the cooked, cold cake with warmed honey and sprinkle with demerara sugar (or coffee crystals) before serving.*
- *Use maple syrup instead of honey.*
- *Add the finely grated rind of 1 lemon or 1 small orange to the mixture before baking.*
- *Use chopped walnuts or ready-to-eat dried apricots instead of dates.*

freezing instructions

Allow to cool completely, then wrap in foil or seal in a freezer bag and label. Freeze for up to 3 months. Defrost thoroughly for several hours at room temperature before serving.

peaches *and* cream

FEED YOUR FACE *with this skin- and nail-boosting menu chosen from the skin and nail foods section. Vitamin and mineral deficiencies will manifest as pallid, dull skin and brittle nails, so eat the right foods to help ensure that healthier nails and a more glowing complexion will be yours!*

shredded beetroot *and* carrot salad

Beetroot contains numerous vitamins and minerals that can help improve the condition of your skin.

ingredients

- 350g (12oz) carrots
- 225g (8oz) raw beetroot
- 115g (4oz) mixed dark-green salad leaves, such as spinach, watercress, lollo rosso (coral lettuce), red (ruby) chard and rocket
- 2tbsp chopped fresh mixed herbs
- 25–55g (1–2oz) toasted hazelnuts, roughly chopped

for the dressing

- 2tbsp hazelnut oil
- 1tbsp olive oil
- juice of 1 lemon
- 1tbsp honey
- 1 clove garlic, crushed
- sea salt
- freshly ground black pepper

serves *four*
preparation time *15 minutes*

method

1 Peel and coarsely grate or shred the carrots and beetroot. Put in a bowl.
2 Add the salad leaves and mixed herbs, and toss. Divide the salad between four serving plates.
3 Put the oils, lemon juice, honey, garlic and seasoning in a bowl and whisk until well mixed.
4 Drizzle the dressing over the salads and toss to mix.
5 Scatter with chopped hazelnuts, and serve immediately, with crusty wholemeal bread.

turkey *and* brussels sprouts stir-fry

The protein and B vitamins in turkey make this main course a real skin helper.

ingredients

- 1tbsp sesame oil
- 350g (12oz) skinless, boneless turkey breast, cut into thin strips
- 1 clove garlic, crushed
- 225g (8oz) Brussels sprouts, shredded
- 1 red pepper (capsicum), seeded and sliced
- 6–8 spring onions, chopped
- 175g (6oz) mushrooms, sliced
- 2tbsp dry sherry
- 2tbsp light soy sauce
- freshly ground black pepper
- 1–2tbsp sunflower seeds

serves *four*
preparation time *15 minutes*
cooking time *8–10 minutes*

method

1 Heat the oil in a non-stick wok or large frying pan. Add the turkey and garlic, and stir-fry over a high heat for 2 minutes.

2 Add the Brussels sprouts and red pepper, and stir-fry for 2–3 minutes.

3 Add the spring onions and mushrooms, and stir-fry for a further 2–3 minutes.

4 Add the sherry, soy sauce and black pepper, and stir-fry until the mixture is piping hot and the turkey and vegetables are cooked and tender.

5 Scatter the turkey with sunflower seeds.

6 Serve with brown rice or rice noodles.

poached pears *with* blackcurrant sauce

The vitamin C in blackcurrants (important for healthy skin and the manufacture of collagen) make this a nutritious dessert.

ingredients

- 300ml (½ pint) unsweetened apple juice or grape juice
- 85g (3oz) dark brown sugar
- 6 ripe pears, peeled and left whole with stalks intact
- pared rind of 1 lemon
- 1 cinnamon stick, broken in half
- 6 whole cloves
- 225g (8oz) fresh or frozen (defrosted) blackcurrants
- 2tsp arrowroot
- 2tbsp crème de cassis or blackcurrant liqueur
- fresh mint sprigs, to decorate

serves *six*
preparation time *10 minutes*
cooking time *40 minutes*

method

1 Put the apple or grape juice and sugar in a saucepan and heat gently until the sugar has dissolved, stirring continuously.

2 Add the pears, lemon rind, cinnamon stick and cloves, and stir. Cover, bring to the boil, then reduce the heat and simmer for about 15 minutes, until the pears are cooked and tender.

3 Using a slotted spoon, transfer the pears to a serving dish. Cover and keep them warm.

4 Remove and discard the lemon rind, cinnamon stick and cloves.

5 Add the blackcurrants to the pan, cover, bring to the boil, then reduce the heat and simmer for about 10 minutes, until soft, stirring occasionally.

6 Blend the arrowroot with the crème de cassis or liqueur and stir into the blackcurrant sauce. Heat gently, stirring continuously, until the sauce comes to the boil and thickens slightly.

7 Pour the sauce over the pears and decorate with the mint sprigs.

8 Serve warm or cold with plain yoghurt or home-made yoghurt ice.

hair *foods*

The condition of your hair is often an indication of your general health and well-being. People suffering from physical stress may be short of B vitamins, which are essential for healthy hair. A deficiency of vitamin A may cause dry hair, so you should ensure that your diet includes plenty of carrots, dark-green leafy vegetables, red sweet potatoes and apricots. Abnormal hair loss and a dry scalp may signal a severe zinc deficiency – foods rich in zinc include seafood, poultry, eggs, grains and pulses.

spicy carrot *and* barley soup

This hot spicy soup, served with crusty wholemeal bread or rolls, is great for chilly winter days. Carrots provide beta carotene, which the body converts into vitamin A, a nutrient important for healthy hair.

ingredients

- 1tbsp olive oil
- 1 onion, finely chopped
- 450g (1lb) carrots, finely chopped
- 2 sticks celery, finely chopped
- 55g (2oz) pearl barley
- 2tsp ground cumin
- 2tsp ground coriander
- 1tsp hot chilli powder (optional)
- 850ml (1½ pints) vegetable stock (see recipe on page 20)
- sea salt
- freshly ground black pepper
- fresh chopped parsley, to garnish

serves *four*
preparation time *10 minutes*
cooking time *1¼ hours*

method

1 Heat the oil in a large saucepan. Add the onion and cook for 5 minutes, stirring occasionally.
2 Add the carrots, celery, pearl barley and ground spices. Cook for 1 minute, stirring continuously. Stir in the stock.
3 Cover, bring to the boil, then reduce the heat and simmer for about 1¼ hours, stirring occasionally, until the barley is cooked and tender. Season to taste with salt and pepper.
4 Ladle into warmed soup bowls and garnish with the parsley.
5 Serve with wholemeal bread.

variations

- *Omit the barley, if preferred. Cook the soup as directed for about 45 minutes, then purée in a blender or food processor until smooth. Reheat before serving.*
- *Use 1 large leek instead of the onion.*
- *Use parsnips or swede instead of carrots.*

freezing instructions

Allow to cool completely, then transfer to a rigid, freezeproof container. Cover, seal and label. Freeze for up to 3 months. Defrost, and reheat gently in a saucepan until piping hot.

melon *and* prawn starter

Melons filled with prawns tossed in a light dressing make a popular starter. Orange-fleshed melons are the most nutritious of the many varieties of melon. They are a rich source of vitamin A (via beta carotene), which is an excellent hair food.

ingredients

- 2 small cantaloupe (orange-fleshed) melons
- 350g (12oz) cooked, peeled prawns
- fresh parsley sprigs, to garnish

for the dressing

- 4tbsp mayonnaise (see recipe on page 21)
- 2tbsp plain yoghurt
- 2tbsp chopped fresh parsley
- 1tsp finely grated lemon rind
- sea salt
- freshly ground black pepper

serves *four*
preparation time *15 minutes*

method

1 Halve the melons and remove and discard the seeds. Place each half on a serving plate.

2 Put the mayonnaise, yoghurt, chopped parsley, lemon rind and seasoning in a bowl and stir. Fold in the prawns and mix well.

3 Pile the prawn mixture into the melon halves and garnish with the parsley sprigs.

4 Serve with fingers of lightly buttered wholemeal bread.

variations

- *Use fresh flaked crab, or canned tuna or salmon, instead of prawns.*
- *Use avocados instead of melons.*
- *Use chopped fresh coriander instead of parsley.*
- *Use grated lime rind instead of lemon rind.*

spinach *and* avocado salad

A combination of spinach leaves and avocados, tossed together in a flavoursome nutty dressing, makes a delicious starter. Spinach is rich in antioxidants, such as beta carotene and vitamin C.

ingredients

- 175g (6oz) baby spinach leaves
- half a cucumber, sliced
- 4 sticks celery, chopped
- 2 large, ripe avocados
- juice of 1 lemon

for the dressing

- 4tbsp hazelnut or olive oil
- 2–3tsp balsamic vinegar
- 1 clove garlic, crushed
- 1tsp honey
- 1tbsp chopped fresh parsley
- 1tbsp chopped fresh chives
- sea salt
- freshly ground black pepper

serves *six*
preparation time *15 minutes*

method

1 Put the spinach leaves, cucumber and celery in a bowl.

2 Peel, stone, and slice or chop the avocados and toss them in the lemon juice. Add to the salad and stir gently to mix.

3 Put all the dressing ingredients in a bowl and whisk together. Drizzle over the salad and toss gently to mix.

4 Serve immediately, with wholemeal bread.

variations

- *Use 2 courgettes (zucchini) instead of the cucumber.*
- *Use 1 small green pepper (capsicum), seeded and diced, instead of celery.*
- *Use 1 medium cantaloupe (orange-fleshed) melon instead of the avocados.*

tagliatelle *with* salmon, courgettes *and* almonds

Freshly cooked pasta served with a salmon and courgette (zucchini) sauce, topped with toasted almonds is a delicious and nutritious meal. Almonds are a good source of vitamins E and B_2 and minerals such as magnesium and phosphorus.

ingredients

- 25g (1oz) butter
- 225g (8oz) leeks, washed and thinly sliced
- 225g (8oz) courgettes (zucchini), thinly sliced
- 25g (1oz) plain wholemeal flour
- 425ml (¾ pint) vegetable stock (see recipe on page 20)
- 150ml (¼ pint) dry white wine
- 400g can (14oz can) salmon in water, drained and flaked
- 1–2tbsp chopped fresh tarragon
- dash of Tabasco sauce
- sea salt
- freshly ground black pepper
- 350g (12oz) tagliatelle
- 55g (2oz) toasted flaked almonds
- fresh tarragon sprigs, to garnish

serves *four*
preparation time *10 minutes*
cooking time *20 minutes*

method

1 Melt the butter in a saucepan and add the leeks and courgettes. Cover and cook gently for about 10 minutes, until softened, stirring occasionally.

2 Add the flour and cook gently for 1 minute, stirring. Gradually stir in the stock and wine, then bring slowly to the boil, stirring continuously, until the sauce thickens. Simmer gently for 2 minutes, stirring.

3 Stir the salmon, chopped tarragon, Tabasco sauce and seasoning into the sauce. Reheat gently until piping hot, stirring.

4 Meanwhile, cook the pasta in a large saucepan of lightly salted, boiling water until *al dente*.

5 Drain the pasta well and transfer to serving plates. Spoon the sauce over the pasta and scatter with almonds. Garnish with the tarragon sprigs.

6 Serve with a mixed dark-green leafy salad.

variations

- *Use 1 onion instead of leeks.*
- *Use canned tuna instead of salmon.*
- *Use fresh parsley or coriander instead of tarragon.*

baked trout *with* lemon *and* almonds

Trout is delicious baked with lemon juice and almonds. Oily fish such as trout provide vitamins A and D, and omega-3 fatty acids, all of which are good hair nutrients.

ingredients

- 4 rainbow trout, each weighing about 280g (10oz), gutted and cleaned, with heads and tails left on
- finely grated rind and juice of 2 lemons
- 40g (1½oz) butter, melted
- 3tbsp chopped fresh parsley
- sea salt
- freshly ground black pepper
- 55g (2oz) flaked almonds

serves *four*
preparation time *10 minutes*
cooking time *25–30 minutes*

method

1 Preheat the oven to 180°C/350°F/gas mark 4.
2 Make three diagonal slashes on both sides of each fish and place in a shallow ovenproof dish.
3 Mix together the lemon rind and juice, melted butter, parsley and seasoning. Pour over the fish and scatter with almonds.
4 Cover the fish with foil and bake for 25–30 minutes, until the flesh just flakes when tested with a fork.
5 Serve with sautéed potatoes and cooked fresh vegetables, such as peas and shredded green cabbage.

variations

- *Use mackerel or any other oily fish instead of trout.*
- *Use 2 limes or 1 orange instead of lemons.*
- *Use fresh chives or coriander instead of parsley.*

braised lamb's liver *with* apples

This tender, oven-braised lamb's liver, topped with apples, is served with a tasty sauce. Lamb's liver is one of the best sources of vitamin A, folate and iron, and also provides selenium – all essential nutrients for healthy hair.

ingredients

- 1tbsp olive oil
- 450g (1lb) lamb's liver, thinly sliced
- 1 leek, washed and sliced
- 2 eating apples, peeled, cored and thinly sliced
- 1tbsp cornflour
- 150ml (¼ pint) unsweetened apple juice
- 150ml (¼ pint) vegetable stock (see recipe on page 20)
- 1tbsp wholegrain mustard
- 1tsp dried *herbes de provence*
- sea salt
- freshly ground black pepper
- fresh herb sprigs, to garnish

serves *four to six*
preparation time *20 minutes*
cooking time *20–25 minutes*

method

1 Preheat the oven to 190°C/375°F/gas mark 5.

2 Heat the oil in a large non-stick frying pan. Add the liver and cook for about 1 minute on each side, until sealed all over. Using a spatula, transfer the liver to an ovenproof dish. Cover and keep warm.

3 Add the leeks to the pan and cook gently for 5 minutes, stirring occasionally. Spoon over the liver and put the apple slices on top.

4 Blend the cornflour with the apple juice and pour into the pan. Add the stock. Bring to the boil, stirring continuously, until the sauce thickens slightly. Simmer for 1 minute, stirring.

5 Stir in the mustard, dried herbs and seasoning, then pour the sauce over the liver mixture. Cover and bake for 20–25 minutes, until the liver is cooked.

6 Garnish with the herb sprigs and serve with cooked fresh vegetables, such as new potatoes, mangetout (snowpeas) and baby courgettes (zucchini).

variations

- *Use lamb's kidneys instead of liver.*
- *Use pears instead of apples.*
- *Use unsweetened grape juice instead of apple juice.*
- *Leave the apples unpeeled.*

chicken *and* wild mushroom risotto

Chicken and wild mushrooms give this risotto a wonderful flavour. As well as containing dietary fibre, brown rice is an excellent source of magnesium, potassium, B vitamins and selenium.

ingredients

- 1tbsp olive oil
- 225g (8oz) skinless, boneless chicken breast, cut into small pieces
- 1 onion, chopped
- 1 large clove garlic, crushed
- 3 sticks celery, chopped
- 225g (8oz) mixed fresh wild mushrooms, such as shiitake and oyster mushrooms, sliced
- 175g (6oz) frozen petit pois (baby peas)
- 200g (7oz) can sweetcorn kernels, drained
- 225g (8oz) long grain brown rice
- 425ml (¾ pint) chicken stock (see recipe on page 20)
- 425ml (¾ pint) dry white wine
- sea salt
- freshly ground black pepper
- 2–3tbsp chopped fresh mixed herbs
- 25g (1oz) fresh Parmesan cheese, finely grated

serves *four to six*
preparation time *15 minutes*
cooking time *40 minutes*

method

1 Heat the oil in a large saucepan. Add the chicken and cook gently for about 5 minutes, until sealed all over, stirring frequently.

2 Stir in all the remaining ingredients, except the herbs and Parmesan cheese.

3 Bring to the boil, then reduce the heat and cook gently, uncovered, for about 35 minutes, until the rice and chicken are cooked and tender and almost all the liquid has been absorbed, stirring occasionally.

4 Stir in the mixed herbs, and sprinkle with a little Parmesan cheese to serve.

5 Serve with a tomato, pepper (capsicum) and onion salad.

variations

- *Use turkey or lean lamb instead of chicken.*
- *Use button or field mushrooms instead of wild mushrooms.*
- *Use fresh tarragon or coriander instead of mixed herbs.*

freezing instructions

Allow to cool completely, then transfer to a rigid, freezeproof container. Cover, seal and label. Freeze for up to 3 months. Defrost completely, and reheat gently in a saucepan until piping hot, adding a little extra stock, if necessary.

spiced tofu *and* carrot burgers

A tasty vegetarian alternative to meat, these spicy tofu burgers make a great snack or light meal. Tofu is an excellent source of protein and is rich in calcium, magnesium, folate and iron – all of which are needed for healthy hair.

ingredients

- 2tbsp olive oil
- 6 shallots (French shallots), finely chopped
- 175g (6oz) carrots, coarsely grated
- 1 clove garlic, crushed
- 1½tsp ground coriander
- 1½tsp ground cumin
- ½tsp hot chilli powder
- 350g (12oz) tofu, mashed
- 55g (2oz) ground almonds
- 55g (2oz) Cheddar cheese, finely grated
- 1tbsp sun-dried tomato purée (paste)
- 1tbsp chopped fresh coriander
- sea salt
- freshly ground black pepper

serves *four (two burgers each)*
preparation time *20 minutes*
cooking time *8 minutes*

method

1 Heat 1tbsp oil in a saucepan. Add the shallots, carrots and garlic, and cook over a medium heat for 4 minutes, stirring occasionally. Add the ground spices and cook for 1 minute, stirring.

2 Turn the mixture into a bowl. Add the tofu, almonds, cheese, tomato purée, coriander and seasoning, and mix well. Cool slightly, then divide the mixture into eight portions and form each portion into a burger.

3 Preheat the grill to high. Brush each burger all over with the remaining oil and place the burgers on a rack in a grill pan.

4 Grill for about 4 minutes on each side, until cooked and lightly browned.

5 Serve with wholemeal bread rolls, home-made relish or chutney, and a mixed leaf salad.

variations

- *Use coarsely grated courgettes (zucchini) instead of carrots.*
- *Use hazelnuts instead of almonds.*

chewy fruit *and* nut bars

These chewy bars are ideal for a packed lunch. Dried fruits and oats provide dietary fibre and a number of essential hair nutrients.

ingredients

- 175g (6oz) butter
- 175g (6oz) light brown sugar
- 3tbsp maple syrup
- 250g (9oz) rolled oats
- 2tsp ground cinnamon
- 140g (5oz) mixed dried fruit, including sultanas, raisins, and chopped dried apricots and peaches
- 85g (3oz) mixed almonds and hazelnuts, chopped

makes *16 bars*
preparation time *20 minutes*
cooking time *20–25 minutes*

method

1 Preheat the oven to 180°C/350°F/gas mark 4.

2 Lightly grease an 18x28cm (7x11in) cake tin.

3 Put the butter, sugar and syrup in a saucepan and heat gently until melted, stirring occasionally. Remove from the heat.

4 Stir in the oats, cinnamon, dried fruit and nuts, and mix well.

5 Turn the mixture into the tin and press down to level the surface. Bake for 20–25 minutes, or until golden brown.

6 Mark into bars while still warm and leave to cool in the tin. Break into bars and serve.

variations

- *Use honey instead of maple syrup.*
- *Use ground mixed spice or ginger instead of cinnamon.*
- *Use cashew and Brazil nuts instead of almonds and hazelnuts.*

freezing instructions

Allow to cool completely, then wrap in foil or seal in a freezer bag and label. Freeze for up to 3 months. Defrost thoroughly for several hours at room temperature before serving.

banana *and* apricot compote

This simple compote of apricots and bananas is delicious served with plain yoghurt. Bananas are easy to digest and are a good source of potassium and magnesium.

ingredients

- 200ml (7fl oz) unsweetened apple juice
- 200ml (7fl oz) unsweetened orange juice
- 4tbsp brandy
- 2tbsp honey
- 225g (8oz) small ready-to-eat dried apricots
- 2 cinnamon sticks, broken in half
- 6 whole cloves
- 4 firm, ripe bananas

serves *four*
preparation time *10 minutes*
cooking time *25 minutes*

method

1 Put the fruit juices, brandy and honey in a saucepan and stir. Add the apricots, cinnamon sticks and cloves, and bring to the boil. Reduce the heat, cover and simmer for 20 minutes, stirring occasionally. Remove the pan from the heat and discard the whole spices.
2 Peel and slice the bananas diagonally, add to the pan and stir.
3 Serve immediately, or set aside to cool and refrigerate before serving.
4 Serve with plain yoghurt, crème fraîche, light sour cream or home-made yoghurt ice.

variations

- *Use unsweetened pineapple or grape juice instead of apple juice.*
- *Use chopped ready-to-eat dried peaches, pears or pineapple instead of apricots.*
- *Use sherry or rum instead of brandy.*

great *hair* day

DINE YOUR WAY *to a healthier head of hair with delicious recipes from the hair foods section – all include essential hair nutrients. Stress and pollution take their toll on our hair, so we need to ensure that we nourish our hair and scalp from the inside as well as caring for it on the outside.*

spicy carrot *and* barley soup

Carrots provide beta carotene, which the body converts to vitamin A, an important nutrient for healthy hair.

ingredients

- 1tbsp olive oil
- 1 onion, finely chopped
- 450g (1lb) carrots, finely chopped
- 2 sticks celery, finely chopped
- 55g (2oz) pearl barley
- 2tsp ground cumin
- 2tsp ground coriander
- 1tsp hot chilli powder (optional)
- 850ml (1½ pints) vegetable stock (see recipe on page 20)
- sea salt
- freshly ground black pepper
- fresh chopped parsley, to garnish

serves *four*
preparation time *10 minutes*
cooking time *1¼ hours*

method

1 Heat the oil in a large saucepan. Add the onion and cook for 5 minutes, stirring occasionally.
2 Add the carrots, celery, pearl barley and ground spices. Cook for 1 minute, stirring continuously. Stir in the stock.
3 Cover, bring to the boil, then reduce the heat and simmer for about 1¼ hours, stirring occasionally, until the barley is cooked and tender. Season to taste with salt and pepper.
4 Ladle into warmed soup bowls and garnish with the parsley.
5 Serve with wholemeal bread.

chicken *and* wild mushroom risotto

The brown rice – excellent source of magnesium, potassium, vitamins B_3 and E, folate and selenium – will encourage a shining head of hair and healthy scalp.

ingredients

- 1tbsp olive oil
- 225g (8oz) skinless, boneless chicken breast, cut into small pieces
- 1 onion, chopped
- 1 large clove garlic, crushed
- 3 sticks celery, chopped
- 225g (8oz) mixed fresh wild mushrooms, such as shiitake and oyster mushrooms, sliced
- 175g (6oz) frozen petit pois (baby peas)
- 200g (7oz) can sweetcorn kernels, drained
- 225g (8oz) long grain brown rice
- 425ml (¾ pint) chicken stock (see recipe on page 20)
- 425ml (¾ pint) dry white wine
- sea salt
- freshly ground black pepper
- 2–3tbsp chopped fresh mixed herbs
- 25g (1oz) fresh Parmesan cheese, finely grated

serves *four to six*
preparation time *15 minutes*
cooking time *40 minutes*

method

1 Heat the oil in a large saucepan. Add the chicken and cook gently for about 5 minutes, until sealed all over, stirring frequently.
2 Stir in all the remaining ingredients, except the herbs and Parmesan cheese.
3 Bring to the boil, then reduce the heat and cook gently, uncovered, for about 35 minutes, until the rice and chicken are cooked and tender and almost all the liquid has been absorbed, stirring occasionally.
4 Stir in the mixed herbs, and sprinkle with a little Parmesan cheese to serve.
5 Serve with a tomato, pepper (capsicum) and onion salad.

banana *and* apricot compote

Bananas are a good source of potassium, magnesium and iron.

ingredients

- 200ml (7fl oz) unsweetened apple juice
- 200ml (7fl oz) unsweetened orange juice
- 4tbsp brandy
- 2tbsp honey
- 225g (8oz) small ready-to-eat dried apricots
- 2 cinnamon sticks, broken in half
- 6 whole cloves
- 4 firm, ripe bananas

serves *four*
preparation time *10 minutes*
cooking time *25 minutes*

method

1 Put the fruit juices, brandy and honey in a saucepan and stir. Add the apricots, cinnamon sticks and cloves, and bring to the boil. Reduce the heat, cover and simmer for 20 minutes, stirring occasionally. Remove the pan from the heat and discard the whole spices.
2 Peel and slice the bananas diagonally, add to the pan and stir.
3 Serve immediately, or set aside to cool and chill before serving.
4 Serve with plain yoghurt, crème fraîche, light sour cream or home-made yoghurt ice.

vision *foods*

FOODS THAT ARE *rich in vitamin A and beta carotene (the plant form of vitamin A), such as lamb's liver, oily fish, carrots, spinach, and apricots, are essential for healthy eyes. A deficiency of vitamin A results in night blindness and dry eyes. Insufficient vitamin B_2 can lead to inflamed eyelids and sensitivity to light. Vitamin B_2 is found in foods such as milk, yoghurt, leafy green vegetables, eggs, meat, poultry and fish. The omega-3 group of fatty acids, found in oily fish and walnuts, is also very important for healthy eyes.*

mixed leaf *and* herb salad *with* grilled haloumi

This simple salad of mixed dark-green leaves and fresh herbs, topped with grilled haloumi cheese, makes a tasty starter. Spinach is rich in beta carotene, which is important for vision.

ingredients

- 115g (4oz) mixed dark-green salad leaves, such as baby spinach, rocket and lollo rosso (coral lettuce)
- 55g (2oz) watercress
- 15g (½oz) fresh herbs, such as parsley, basil, tarragon, mint and chives, roughly torn or chopped
- 225g (8oz) cherry tomatoes, halved
- 1tbsp olive oil
- 1tbsp lemon juice
- 250g (9oz) haloumi cheese, thinly sliced

for the dressing

- 3tbsp walnut oil
- 2tsp white wine vinegar
- 1tsp honey
- 1tsp Dijon mustard
- sea salt
- freshly ground black pepper

serves *four*
preparation time *15 minutes*
cooking time *6–8 minutes*

method

1 Put the salad leaves, watercress, herbs and tomatoes in a bowl and toss together.

2 To make the dressing, put the walnut oil, vinegar, honey, mustard and seasoning in a bowl and whisk. Drizzle over the salad and toss to mix. Divide the salad between four serving plates.

3 Preheat the grill to high. Cover a grill rack with foil. Mix together the olive oil and lemon juice, and brush over the haloumi cheese.

4 Place the cheese on the rack and grill for 3–4 minutes each side, until lightly browned.

5 Top each salad with cheese slices and serve immediately, with wholemeal bread.

variations

- *Use watercress instead of rocket.*
- *Use olive oil or hazelnut oil instead of walnut oil.*
- *Use button mushrooms, halved, instead of tomatoes.*

mushroom *and* asparagus frittata

This delicious frittata makes a substantial starter or snack. Asparagus contains carotenoids, which are important for vision.

ingredients

- 115g (4oz) asparagus tips
- 15g (½oz) butter
- 1 leek, washed and sliced
- 115g (4oz) mushrooms, sliced
- 4 medium eggs, beaten
- 55g (2oz) Cheddar cheese, grated
- sea salt
- freshly ground black pepper
- 2 tomatoes, skinned, seeded and chopped
- fresh herb sprigs, to garnish

serves *two*
preparation time *10 minutes*
cooking time *15 minutes*

method

1 Cook the asparagus in a saucepan of boiling water for about 2 minutes, until cooked and tender. Drain well and keep warm.

2 Melt the butter in a medium-sized non-stick frying pan. Add the leeks and mushrooms, and cook gently for 8–10 minutes, until softened, stirring occasionally.

3 Preheat the grill to high. Pour the eggs over the vegetables in the pan, sprinkle with cheese and seasoning, and stir briefly.

4 Cook over a medium heat for a few minutes, until cooked and golden brown underneath.

5 Put under the grill for a few minutes to brown the top.

6 Scatter the asparagus and tomatoes on top and serve on its own or with wholemeal bread or toast. Garnish with the herb sprigs.

variations

- *Add 1tbsp chopped fresh or 1tsp dried mixed herbs to the eggs.*
- *Use sliced courgettes (zucchini) instead of asparagus.*
- *Use 1 onion instead of the leek.*
- *Use 25–55g (1–2oz) fresh Parmesan cheese instead of Cheddar cheese.*

barbecued mackerel *with* mustard sauce

This barbecued mackerel with mustard sauce makes a wonderful alfresco meal. Oily fish such as mackerel contain omega-3 fatty acids and vitamin A, which help to protect cell membranes.

ingredients

- 2 eating apples, peeled, cored and thinly sliced
- 3tbsp chopped fresh parsley
- sea salt
- freshly ground black pepper
- 4 mackerel, each weighing 280–350g (10–12oz), gutted and cleaned
- juice of 2 lemons

for the sauce

- 2tbsp cornflour
- 300ml (½ pint) milk
- 1tbsp wholegrain mustard
- 15g (½oz) butter
- fresh parsley sprigs, to garnish

serves *four*
preparation time *15 minutes*
cooking time *20–30 minutes*

method

1 Heat the barbecue in readiness.
2 Lightly grease four sheets of foil, each large enough to wrap a fish.
3 Mix the apples, 2tbsp chopped parsley and seasoning. Spoon into the fish cavities.
4 Place a fish on each piece of foil, sprinkle with a little lemon juice, then fold the foil over and twist the edges to secure, making four parcels.
5 Cook the parcels on the barbecue for 20–30 minutes, until the flesh just flakes when tested with a fork. (When opening the parcels to check, beware of steam.)
6 Meanwhile, make the sauce. In a saucepan, blend the cornflour with a little milk. Stir in the remaining milk, then heat, stirring, until the sauce comes to the boil and thickens slightly. Simmer for 2 minutes, stirring continuously.
7 Stir in the mustard, butter, seasoning and remaining chopped parsley. Heat gently until piping hot, stirring continuously.
8 Unwrap the fish carefully, place on warmed serving plates and garnish with the parsley sprigs. Pour some sauce over each fish.
9 Serve with baked potatoes, grilled peppers (capsicums) and aubergines (eggplants).

variations

- *Add an extra 1tbsp wholegrain mustard to the sauce if you prefer a slightly stronger mustard flavour.*
- *Use trout instead of mackerel.*
- *Use pears instead of apples.*
- *Use 1–2tbsp finely chopped capers instead of mustard.*

pan-fried squid *with* chilli sauce

Fresh squid, pan-fried and tossed in a hot chilli sauce, makes a tasty meal. Squid is a low-fat source of protein and also contains many other important nutrients. Chillies are an excellent source of vitamin C.

ingredients

- 400g (14oz) can tomatoes, chopped
- 2 shallots (French shallots), finely chopped
- 2 sticks celery, finely chopped
- 1 fresh red chilli, seeded and finely chopped
- 1 clove garlic, crushed
- 150ml (¼ pint) dry white wine
- 1tbsp tomato purée (paste)
- sea salt
- freshly ground black pepper
- 30ml (2tbsp) olive oil
- 900g (2lb) prepared squid, cut into rings

serves *four to six*
Preparation time *10 minutes*
Cooking time *15–20 minutes*

method

1 Put the tomatoes, shallots, celery, chilli, garlic, wine, tomato purée and seasoning in a small saucepan and stir.

2 Bring the mixture to the boil, then reduce the heat to medium and cook, uncovered, for 15–20 minutes, until the sauce is cooked and thickened, stirring occasionally.

3 Meanwhile, heat the olive oil in a non-stick wok or large frying pan. Add the squid and stir-fry over a high heat for 3–5 minutes, until tender.

4 Toss the squid and chilli sauce together and serve with lightly buttered wholemeal bread and a mixed pepper (capsicum) and onion salad.

variations

- *Use red wine or unsweetened apple juice instead of white wine.*
- *Use 1–2tsp hot chilli powder instead of the fresh chilli.*
- *Use 450g (1lb) fresh tomatoes, skinned and chopped, instead of canned tomatoes.*

lamb's liver *with* Madeira sauce

Lamb's liver is an excellent source of vitamins A and B_{12}, folate and iron, but since it's also high in saturated fat and cholesterol, we save it for special occasions.

ingredients

- 1tbsp olive oil
- 6 shallots (French shallots), sliced
- 450g (1lb) lamb's liver, cut into thin strips
- 4tbsp vegetable stock (see recipe on page 20)
- 4tbsp Madeira
- 1tsp dried *herbes de provence*
- 2tbsp crème fraîche or light sour cream
- sea salt
- freshly ground black pepper
- fresh herb sprigs, to garnish

serves *four to six*
preparation time *10 minutes*
cooking time *12 minutes*

method

1 Heat the oil in a large non-stick frying pan. Add the shallots and cook for 5 minutes, stirring.
2 Add the liver and cook over a medium to high heat for 4–5 minutes, stirring frequently.
3 Add the stock, Madeira and dried herbs. Bring to the boil and cook for 1–2 minutes, stirring frequently, until the liver is cooked and tender.
4 Stir in the crème fraîche or light sour cream and seasoning. Reheat gently until piping hot, stirring continuously.
5 Garnish with the herb sprigs.
6 Serve with a mixture of brown and wild rice and cooked fresh vegetables, such as broccoli florets and green beans.

variations

- *Use 1 onion instead of the shallots.*
- *Use lamb's kidneys instead of liver.*
- *Use red wine instead of Madeira.*

chicken *and* broccoli pasta bake

The whole family will enjoy this tasty pasta bake. Broccoli is rich in beta carotene (the plant form of vitamin A), making it an excellent dish to help keep eyes healthy. Chicken is a good source of vitamin B_2.

ingredients

- 225g (8oz) pasta shapes
- 225g (8oz) small broccoli florets
- 2 courgettes (zucchini), sliced
- 1 leek, washed and sliced
- 55g (2oz) butter
- 55g (2oz) plain wholemeal flour
- 600ml (1 pint) chicken stock (see recipe on page 20), cooled
- 300ml (½ pint) milk
- 115g (4oz) Cheddar cheese, grated
- 225g (8oz) cooked skinless, boneless chicken, diced
- 2tbsp chopped fresh chives
- 1tbsp chopped fresh parsley
- sea salt
- freshly ground black pepper
- 2tbsp finely grated fresh Parmesan cheese
- fresh parsley sprigs, to garnish

serves *four to six*
preparation time *20 minutes*
cooking time *25–30 minutes*

method

1 Preheat the oven to 200°C/400°F/gas mark 6.

2 Cook the pasta in a large saucepan of lightly salted, boiling water until *al dente*. Rinse, drain well and keep warm.

3 Meanwhile, steam the broccoli, courgettes (zucchini) and leeks over a saucepan of boiling water for about 10 minutes, until just cooked and tender. Drain well and keep warm.

4 Put the butter, flour, stock and milk in a saucepan and heat gently, whisking continuously, until the sauce comes to the boil and thickens. Simmer gently for 3 minutes, stirring.

5 Remove the pan from the heat and stir in the Cheddar cheese, chicken, chopped herbs and seasoning. Add the pasta and vegetables, and mix well.

6 Spoon the mixture into an ovenproof dish and sprinkle with Parmesan cheese. Bake, uncovered, for 25–30 minutes, until golden brown.

7 Garnish with the parsley sprigs and serve with grilled tomatoes and peppers (capsicums).

variations

- *Use cooked turkey or cooked, flaked salmon or tuna instead of chicken.*
- *Use cauliflower florets or sliced mushrooms instead of broccoli.*
- *Use 1 onion instead of the leek.*

freezing instructions

Allow to cool completely, then transfer to a rigid, freezeproof container. Cover, seal and label. Freeze for up to 3 months. Defrost, and reheat in a moderate oven until hot.

sweet potato wedges *with* sesame seeds

These sweet potato wedges sprinkled with sesame seeds make a tasty accompaniment to many dishes. Sesame seeds are rich in essential fatty acids, and add a little zinc, potassium, magnesium and iron to the diet.

ingredients

- 700g (1lb 9oz) red sweet potatoes
- 1tbsp olive oil
- 15g (½oz) butter
- 2tbsp sesame seeds
- 2tbsp chopped fresh chives
- sea salt
- freshly ground black pepper

serves *four*
preparation time *10 minutes*
cooking time *11–16 minutes*

method

1 Peel the potatoes and cut them into wedges. Parboil in a saucepan of boiling water for 5 minutes. Drain well.

2 Heat the oil and butter in a non-stick frying pan, until the butter has melted. Add the potatoes and cook over a medium heat for about 10–15 minutes, turning occasionally, until the potatoes are cooked, lightly browned and crisp all over.

3 Add the sesame seeds and cook gently for 1–2 minutes, then stir in the chives and seasoning.

4 Serve with grilled lean meat or fish and cooked vegetables, such as spinach and leeks.

variations

- *Use potatoes, parsnips or swede instead of sweet potatoes.*
- *Use sesame oil instead of olive oil.*
- *Use sunflower or pumpkin seeds instead of sesame seeds.*
- *Use chopped fresh mixed herbs instead of chives.*

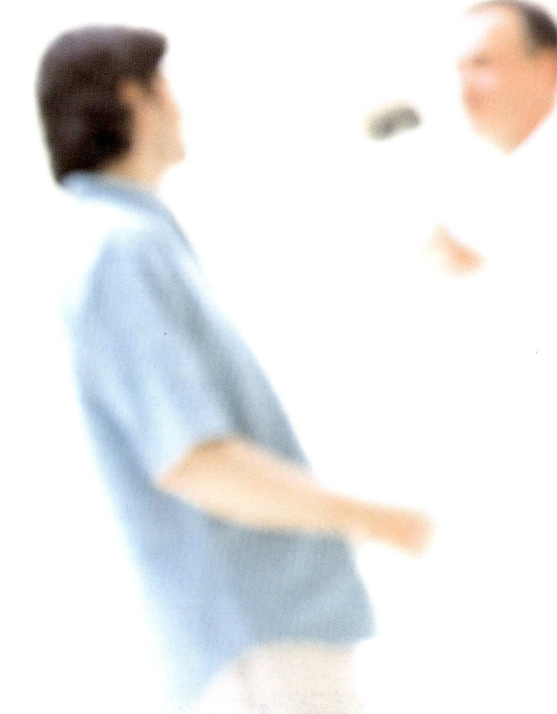

country bean goulash

This hearty goulash makes a delicious, warming meal. Beans and pulses are rich in vitamin B_2, a nutrient that may help prevent cataracts. The vitamin C in tomatoes and red peppers may also have cataract-preventing properties.

ingredients

- 700g (1lb 9oz) tomatoes, skinned, seeded and chopped
- 1 onion, chopped
- 1 large clove garlic, finely chopped
- 1 red pepper (capsicum), seeded and diced
- 3 carrots, sliced
- 3 sticks celery, chopped
- 175g (6oz) button mushrooms
- 175g (6oz) frozen broad beans
- 400g (14oz) can red kidney beans, rinsed and drained
- 400g (14oz) can black-eye beans, rinsed and drained
- 300ml (½ pint) medium sweet cider
- 2tbsp paprika
- 2tsp dried *herbes de provence*
- sea salt
- freshly ground black pepper
- 1tbsp cornflour
- fresh herb sprigs, to garnish

serves *four to six*
preparation time *15 minutes*
cooking time *1½ hours*

method

1 Preheat the oven to 180°C/350°F/gas mark 4.
2 Put all the ingredients, except the cornflour and herb garnish, in a large flameproof, ovenproof casserole dish and stir to mix.
3 Bake for about 1½ hours, until the vegetables are cooked and tender, stirring occasionally. Remove from the oven.
4 Blend the cornflour with 4tbsp water. Stir into the vegetable mixture, then heat gently on top of the stove, stirring continuously, until the mixture comes to the boil and thickens slightly. Simmer gently for 2 minutes, stirring.
5 Serve with brown rice, rice noodles or couscous. Garnish with the herb sprigs.

variations

- *Use unsweetened apple juice instead of cider.*
- *Use peas instead of broad beans.*
- *Use a 400g (14oz) can tomatoes, chopped, instead of fresh tomatoes.*

freezing instructions

Allow to cool completely, then transfer to a rigid, freezeproof container. Cover, seal and label. Freeze for up to 3 months. Defrost, and reheat gently in a saucepan or moderate oven until piping hot.

apricot yoghurt crush

This yoghurt crush, with its delicate, fruity flavour, makes a delicious light dessert. Yoghurt is rich in vitamins B_1 and B_2 and provides easily digestible protein as well as magnesium, potassium, zinc and vitamin A – vital nutrients for healthy eyes.

ingredients

- 400g (14oz) can apricots in fruit juice
- 200g (7oz) can apricots in fruit juice
- 300g (11oz) plain yoghurt
- 150ml (¼ pint) single (pouring) cream
- 2tbsp honey
- fresh mint sprigs, to decorate

serves *six*
preparation time *10 minutes, plus freezing time*

method

1 Blend the apricots and juice in a food processor until smooth.
2 Add the yoghurt, cream and honey, and blend until well mixed. Pour into a chilled, shallow, plastic container. Cover and freeze for 1½–2 hours or until mushy.
3 Spoon into a chilled bowl and mash with a fork until smooth. Return to the container, cover and freeze until firm.
4 Transfer to the refrigerator 30 minutes before serving to soften a little. Serve in scoops and decorate with the mint sprigs.
5 Serve with mixed fresh berries, such as strawberries, raspberries, blueberries and blackberries.

variations

- *Use canned peaches or pineapple instead of apricots.*
- *Use crème fraîche or light sour cream instead of single (pouring) cream.*
- *Use maple syrup instead of honey.*

blueberry *and* apple crunch

A combination of blueberries and apples makes this crunchy nut crumble hard to resist. Blueberries are a great eye food because they provide vitamin C and other antioxidants, which are essential to eye health.

ingredients

- 115g (4oz) plain wholemeal flour
- 85g (3oz) medium oatmeal
- 85g (3oz) butter, chopped
- 85g (3oz) light brown sugar
- 55g (2oz) mixed almonds and Brazil nuts, chopped
- 1tsp ground mixed spice
- 350g (12oz) blueberries
- 350g (12oz) eating apples (peeled and cored weight), thinly sliced
- 3tbsp unsweetened apple juice
- 3tbsp honey

serves *four to six*
preparation time *20 minutes*
cooking time *45 minutes*

method

1 Preheat the oven to 180°C/350°F/gas mark 4.
2 Mix the flour and oatmeal in a bowl, then lightly rub in the butter until the mixture resembles coarse breadcrumbs. Stir in the sugar, nuts and mixed spice.
3 Put the blueberries and apples in an ovenproof dish. Mix together the apple juice and honey, and pour over the fruit. Stir.
4 Spoon the crumble mixture evenly over the fruit.
5 Bake for about 45 minutes, or until the fruit is cooked and the topping is golden brown and crunchy.
6 Serve hot or cold with home-made custard or plain yoghurt.

variations

- *Use fresh mixed berries, such as raspberries and blackberries, instead of blueberries.*
- *Use rolled oats instead of oatmeal.*
- *Use brandy or sherry instead of apple juice.*

a *feast* for the *eye*

SEEING IS BELIEVING. *Feast your eyes on this delicious and nutritious menu chosen from the vision foods section. These recipes are packed with vitamins A (via beta carotene) and, B_2 which are important for eye health and may help to prevent cataracts and conjunctivitis.*

mixed leaf *and* herb salad *with* grilled haloumi

Spinach is a good source of beta carotene (for vitamin A) and vitamin B_2 – important for vision.

ingredients

- 115g (4oz) mixed dark-green salad leaves, such as baby spinach, rocket and lollo rosso (coral lettuce)
- 55g (2oz) watercress
- 15g (½oz) fresh herbs, such as parsley, basil, tarragon, mint and chives, roughly torn or chopped
- 225g (8oz) cherry tomatoes, halved
- 1tbsp olive oil
- 1tbsp lemon juice
- 250g (9oz) haloumi cheese, thinly sliced

for the dressing

- 3tbsp walnut oil
- 2tsp white wine vinegar
- 1tsp honey
- 1tsp Dijon mustard
- sea salt
- freshly ground black pepper

serves *four*
preparation time *15 minutes*
cooking time *6–8 minutes*

method

1 Put the salad leaves, watercress, herbs and tomatoes in a bowl and toss together.

2 To make the dressing, put the walnut oil, vinegar, honey, mustard and seasoning in a bowl and whisk. Drizzle over the salad and toss to mix. Divide the salad between four serving plates.

3 Preheat the grill to high. Cover a grill rack with foil. Mix together the olive oil and lemon juice, and brush over the haloumi cheese.

4 Place the cheese on the rack and grill for 3–4 minutes each side, until lightly browned.

5 Top each salad with cheese slices and serve immediately, with wholemeal bread.

country bean goulash

Beans and pulses are rich in vitamin B_2, a nutrient that may help to prevent cataracts.

ingredients

- 700g (1lb 9oz) tomatoes, skinned, seeded and chopped
- 1 onion, chopped
- 1 large clove garlic, finely chopped
- 1 red pepper (capsicum), seeded and diced
- 3 carrots, sliced
- 3 sticks celery, chopped
- 175g (6oz) button mushrooms
- 175g (6oz) frozen broad beans
- 400g (14oz) can red kidney beans, rinsed and drained

- 400g (14oz) can black-eye beans, rinsed and drained
- 300ml (½ pint) medium sweet cider
- 2tbsp paprika
- 2tsp dried *herbes de provence*
- sea salt
- freshly ground black pepper
- 1tbsp cornflour
- fresh herb sprigs, to garnish

serves *four to six*
preparation time *15 minutes*
cooking time *1½ hours*

method

1 Preheat the oven to 180°C/350°F/gas mark 4.
2 Put all the ingredients, except the cornflour and herb garnish, in a large flameproof, ovenproof casserole dish and stir to mix.
3 Bake for about 1½ hours, until the vegetables are cooked and tender, stirring occasionally. Remove from the oven.
4 Blend the cornflour with 4tbsp water. Stir into the vegetable mixture, then heat gently on top of the stove, stirring continuously, until the mixture comes to the boil and thickens slightly. Simmer gently for 2 minutes, stirring.
5 Serve with brown rice, rice noodles or couscous. Garnish with the herb sprigs.

blueberry *and* apple crunch

Blueberries provide vitamin C and other antioxidants, which are essential to eye health.

ingredients

- 115g (4oz) plain wholemeal flour
- 85g (3oz) medium oatmeal
- 85g (3oz) butter, chopped
- 85g (3oz) light brown sugar
- 55g (2oz) mixed almonds and Brazil nuts, chopped
- 1tsp ground mixed spice
- 350g (12oz) blueberries
- 350g (12oz) eating apples (peeled and cored weight), thinly sliced
- 3tbsp unsweetened apple juice
- 3tbsp honey

serves *four to six*
preparation time *20 minutes*
cooking time *45 minutes*

method

1 Preheat the oven to 180°C/350°F/gas mark 4.
2 Mix the flour and oatmeal in a bowl, then lightly rub in the butter until the mixture resembles coarse breadcrumbs. Stir in the sugar, nuts and mixed spice.
3 Put the blueberries and apples in an ovenproof dish. Mix together the apple juice and honey, and pour over the fruit. Stir.
4 Spoon the crumble mixture evenly over the fruit.
5 Bake for about 45 minutes, or until the fruit is cooked and the topping is golden brown and crunchy.
6 Serve hot or cold with home-made custard or plain yoghurt.

which body problem *needs which* food?

immune system problems

- Foods high in vitamin E, such as vegetable oils, leafy green vegetables, wholegrains, nuts and seeds, help protect the immune system.
- When you feel a cold coming on, make a hot drink with lemon juice, a small piece of fresh root ginger and a teaspoon of honey. The lemon juice is rich in vitamin C, the ginger is warming and the honey soothes the throat.
- Garlic and onions may be helpful in alleviating nasal congestion.

teeth and bones problems

- Help prevent tooth decay by finishing a meal with foods that don't harm your teeth. A small amount of cheese is thought to protect enamel by reducing mouth acidity.
- Bleeding gums can be a sign of vitamin C deficiency. Include plenty of fresh fruit and vegetables in your diet.
- Eating plenty of foods rich in calcium and magnesium, plus doing weight-bearing exercise, is the best way of preventing or minimising osteoporosis.

joint problems

- People who suffer from osteoarthritis should ensure their diet is rich in wholegrain cereals and fresh fruit and vegetables to increase their intake of antioxidants.
- Fish oils may be helpful to people suffering from rheumatoid arthritis. Salmon, trout, mackerel, sardines and tuna all contain omega-3 fatty acids, which may have an anti-inflammatory effect on the joints of some arthritis sufferers.
- Painful joints can sometimes be caused by an intolerance to certain foods.

heart and circulation problems

- A diet high in wholegrains, fruit and vegetables helps to lower cholesterol.
- Fats from oily fish such as salmon, trout, mackerel, sardines and tuna can help to prevent blood clots forming in the arteries.
- Garlic and onions eaten regularly may help to lower blood pressure and cholesterol levels.
- If you suffer from high blood pressure, reduce the amount of sodium-based salt in your diet and use unrefined natural sea salt, which is rich in magnesium.

which beauty problem *needs which* food?

skin problems

- If you have a skin rash or hives, or suffer from eczema, it may signal an allergy to particular foods. Common allergens are milk products, nuts, citrus fruits, tomatoes, fish and shellfish, eggs and wheat. The only way that such an allergy can be confirmed is by means of an elimination diet.
- To improve flaking skin, include plenty of essential fatty acids in your diet.
- If you have sensitive skin, or cracks and sores around your mouth, make sure that you eat plenty of foods rich in B vitamins.
- Dabbing fresh lemon juice onto the skin and massaging it in gently with a little extra virgin olive oil is an excellent remedy for improving skin condition and reducing wrinkles.
- If you suffer from acne, eat plenty of fresh fruit and vegetables for vitamin C, as well as foods that contain zinc – such as shellfish, nuts, poultry and lean meat. Cut down on chocolate and sweets, highly salted snacks, and fatty and fried foods. And drink plenty of water.
- Psoriasis sufferers may benefit from increasing their intake of oily fish, for more omega-3 fatty acids.

nail problems

- If you have brittle, flaking nails, include plenty of essential fatty acids in your diet.
- Pale, brittle nails and itchy skin may indicate iron deficiency. Good sources of iron include meat, dark-meat poultry, enriched breads and cereals and green leafy vegetables.
- Brittle nails, infections of the surrounding skin, or white marks on the fingernails may indicate zinc deficiency. Zinc-rich foods include seafood, eggs, liver, nuts, lentils and chickpeas.

hair problems

- Dry scalp and dandruff may indicate a deficiency of zinc, so eat plenty of seafood, eggs, liver, nuts, lentils and chickpeas. Essential fatty acids, found in oily fish, nuts and seeds, also help a dry scalp and dry hair.
- Dull hair may indicate a lack of vitamin A. For beta carotene (the plant form of vitamin A) ensure your diet includes plenty of carrots, dark-green leafy vegetables and dried apricots.

eye problems

- The risk of cataracts and an age-related eye condition known as macular degeneration may be reduced by eating plenty of green leafy vegetables.
- If you suffer from conjunctivitis or bloodshot eyes, ensure you are getting enough Vitamin B_2 – found in meat, eggs, milk, cheese, yoghurt, pulses and green leafy vegetables.
- Poor vision in the dark may be a sign of a deficiency of vitamin A. Ensure your diet includes plenty of carrots, dark-green vegetables and dried apricots.

vitamins *and* minerals

FOODS CONTAIN DIFFERENT *amounts of nutrients, and no single food can provide all the nutrients needed for good health. Vitamins and minerals found in foods work synergistically with proteins, carbohydrates, fats and each other. To make sure you obtain sufficient amounts of all nutrients, vary your diet as much as possible. The following lists are a guide to recommended daily nutritional requirements.*

Fat-soluble vitamins

vitamin A

from retinol in animal products and beta carotene in plant foods

Vital for growth and cell development, vision and immune function. Maintains healthy skin, hair, nails, bones and teeth.

vitamin D

calciferols

Needed for calcium absorption; helps build and maintain strong bones and teeth.

vitamin E

tocopherols

Protects fatty acids; maintains muscles and red blood cells; a major antioxidant.

vitamin K

phylloquinone, menaquinone

Essential for proper blood clotting.

Water-soluble vitamins

biotin

Needed to release energy from food. Important in the synthesis of fat and cholesterol.

folate

folic acid, folacin

Required for cell division and the formation of DNA, RNA and proteins in the body. Extra needed before conception and in pregnancy to protect against neural tube defects.

vitamin B_1

thiamin

Needed to obtain energy from carbohydrates, fats and alcohol; prevents the build up of toxins in the body that may damage the heart and nervous system.

vitamin B_2

riboflavin

Needed to release energy from food and to assist the functioning of vitamin B_6 and niacin.

vitamin B_3

niacin, nicotine acid, nicotinamide

Needed to produce energy in cells. Helps to maintain healthy skin and an efficient digestive system.

vitamin B_5

pantothenic acid

Helps to release energy from food. Essential to the synthesis of cholesterol, fat and red blood cells.

vitamin B_6

pyridoxine, pyridoxamine, pyridoxal

Helps to release energy from proteins; important for immune function, the nervous system and the formation of red blood cells.

vitamin B_{12}

cyanocobalamin

Needed to make red blood cells, DNA, RNA and myelin (for nerve fibres).

vitamin C

ascorbic acid

Vitamin C is a major antioxidant, vital for healthy immune function, and for the production of collagen (a protein essential for healthy gums, teeth, bones, cartilage and skin). It also aids the absorption of iron from plant food.

Minerals

calcium

Builds strong bones and teeth; vital to muscle and nerve function and blood clotting.

chloride

Maintains proper body chemistry. Used to make digestive juices.

chromium

Helps to regulate blood sugar levels and blood cholesterol levels.

copper

Needed for bone growth and connective tissue formation. It helps the body to absorb iron from food and is present in many enzymes that protect against free radicals.

iodine

Necessary for the manufacture of thyroid hormones.

iron

Needed for the manufacture of red blood cells and for energy production within cells.

magnesium

Stimulates bone growth, assists in nerve impulses, and is important for muscle contraction.

manganese

Vital component of various enzymes involved in energy production; helps to form bone and connective tissue.

molybdenum

Essential component of enzymes involved in the production of DNA and RNA; may fight tooth decay.

potassium

Helps to regulate the body's fluid balance and distribution, to keep the heartbeat regular and maintain normal blood pressure. It is important for muscle and nerve function.

phosphorus

Helps maintain strong bones and teeth. However, in excess (such as results from excessive consumption of fizzy drinks) it adversely affects the body's ability to use calcium and magnesium.

selenium

A major antioxidant that works with vitamin E to protect cell membranes from damage due to oxidation.

sodium

Works with potassium to regulate the body's fluid balance; essential for proper nerve and muscle function.

sulphur

Component of two essential amino acids that help to form many proteins in the body.

zinc

Essential for normal growth, reproduction and immune function.

vitamins

	UK		AUSTRALIA AND NEW ZEALAND		SOUTH AFRICA	
	Daily Requirement†		Recommended Dietary Intakes†		Recommended Daily Allowances†	
	MEN	WOMEN	MEN	WOMEN	MEN	WOMEN
Vitamin A	700mcg	600mcg (950mcg in lactation)	750mcg.	750mcg (1200mcg in lactation)	1000mg	800mg (1300mg in lactation)
Vitamin D	Enough vitamin D is made when the skin is exposed to sunlight. People who are confined indoors require about 10 mcg from the diet.					
Vitamin E	At least 4mg	At least 3mg	10mg	7mg	10mg	8mg
Vitamin K	70mcg	65mcg	– *	– *	70–80mcg	60–65mcg
Biotin	10–200mcg	10–200mcg	– *	– *	30–100mcg	30–100mcg
Folate	200mcg	200mcg (400mcg in pregnancy)	200mcg	200mcg (400mcg in pregnancy; 350 mcg in lactation)	200mcg	180mcg (400mcg in pregnancy)
Vitamin B1 (Thiamin)	1mg	0.8mg	1.1mg	0.8mg	1.5mg	1.1mg
Vitamin B2 (Riboflavin)	1.3mg	1.1mg	1.7mg	1.2mg	1.7mg	1.3mg
Vitamin B3 (Niacin)	17mg	13mg	19mg	13mg	19mg	15mg
Vitamin B5 (Pantothenic acid)	3–7mg	3–7mg	– *	– *	4–7mg	4–7mg
Vitamin B6 (Pyridoxine)	1.4mg	1.2mg	1.3–1.9mg	0.9–1.4mg	2.0mg	1.6mg
Vitamin B12 (cyanocobalamin)	1.5mcg	1.5mcg	2mcg	2mcg	2.0mcg	2.0mcg
Vitamin C	40mg (smokers at least 80mg)	40mg	40mg (smokers at least 80mg)	30mg	60mg (smokers at least 80–120mg)	60mg

* *No daily requirement established.*

† *Pregnant and lactating women require a slightly higher intake of most vitamins, and should be guided by their doctor or nutritionist.*

minerals

	UK		AUSTRALIA AND NEW ZEALAND		SOUTH AFRICA	
	Daily Requirement†		Recommended Dietary Intakes†		Recommended Daily Allowances†	
	MEN	WOMEN	MEN	WOMEN	MEN	WOMEN
Calcium	700mg	700mg	800mg	800mg (1000mg after menopause)	800mg	800mg
Chloride	2500mg	2500mg	–*	–*	750mg	750mg
Chromium	25mg	25mg	–*	–*	50–200mg	50–200mg
Copper	1.2mg	1.2mg	–*	–*	1.5–3.0mg	1.5–3.0mg
Iodine	140mcg	140mcg	150mcg	120mcg	150mcg	150mcg
Iron	8.7mg	14. 5mg	7mg	12–16mg (5–7mg after menopause)	10mg	15mg
Magnesium	300mg	270mg	320mg	270mg	350mg	280mg
Manganese	1.4mg	1.4mg	–*	–*	2.0–5.0mg	2.0–5.0mg
Molybdenum	50–400mcg	50–400mcg	–*	–*	75–250mcg	75–250mcg
Phosphorus	550mg	550mg	1000mg	1000mg	800mg	800mg
Potassium	3500mg	3500mg	50–140mmol	50–140mmol	2000mg	2000mg
Selenium	75mg	60mg	85mg	70mg	70mg	55mg
Sodium	1600mg	1600mg	40–100mmol	40–100mmol	500mg	500mg
Sulphur	There is no set dietary requirement in any of these countries					
Zinc	9.5mg	7mg	12mg	12mg	15mg	12mg

† *Pregnant and lactating women require a slightly higher intake of most vitamins, and should be guided by their doctor or nutritionist.*

* *No daily requirement established.*

index

A
almonds *17, 156, 158*
apples *12, 40, 116, 159, 182*
apricots *12, 74, 106, 116, 164, 182*
artichokes *15, 129*
asparagus 15, *46, 72, 170*
avocados *15, 48, 154*

B
bamboo shoots *15*
bananas *12, 62, 108, 149, 164*
beans, broad *128*
beans, dried *16, 96, 180*
beans, green *10, 15, 56, 128*
beauty foods *104–85*
beetroot *14, 158*
bell peppers see *sweet peppers*
blackberries *12*
blackcurrants *12, 146*
blackstrap molasses *17*
blueberries *12, 182*
body *9, 11, 22–103*
bones and teeth *68–87, 186*
brassicas *14*
Brazil nuts *17*
broccoli *10, 14, 46, 92, 136, 176*
Brussels sprouts *48, 142*
butter *11, 16*
buttermilk *16*

C
carambolas *12*
carbohydrates *9, 124–9*
carrots *14, 24, 130, 138, 152*
cashew nuts *17*
celery *14*
cereals *15–16, 18, 98*
cheese *16, 27, 100, 168*
cherries *12, 98*
chicken, see *also meat and poultry dishes*;
  nutritional benefits *15*
  stock *20*
chickpeas *16*
circulation *23, 46–67, 186*
cooking times *19*
couscous *78, 124, 128*
cucumber *113, 140*

D
dairy products *16, 18*
dandelion leaves *14, 114*
defrosting *19*
desserts and bakes
  apricot yoghurt crush *182*
  baked bananas with cinnamon *62*
  banana and apricot compote *164*
  banana and date tealoaf *149*
  blueberry and apple crunch *182*
  cherry buckwheat pancakes *98*
  chewy fruit and nut bars *165*
  chocolate-dipped fruit and nut platter *41*
  exotic dried fruit compote *116*
  fig and apple oat crunchies *40*
  five fruit salad *116*
  fragrant fruit salad *80*
  fruit kebabs with lemon sauce *64*
  fruity breakfast muffins *82*
  marbled cheesecake *100*
  mixed berry yoghurt fool *100*
  pears with blackcurrant sauce *146*
  red fruit jellies *40*
  spicy grilled nectarines *148*
  strawberry yoghurt ice *82*
drinks *106–9*

E
eggs *10, 16, 18, 46, 88, 170*
essential fatty acids *8, 9, 11, 18*
eyes *105, 168–85, 187*

F
fats *8, 10–11*
figs *13, 40, 116*
fish, see *also seafood*
  haddock *52, 119*
  mackerel *72, 172*
  nutritional benefits *15*
  oils *17*
  salmon *30, 72, 156*
  sardines *140*
  trout *90, 158*
  tuna *122*
freezing *19*
French dressing *21*
fruit, see *also desserts and bakes*;
  soups and starters
  in diet *9, 11*
  dried *13, 40, 116, 149, 165*
  drinks *106–9*
  nutritional benefits *12–13*

G
garlic *14*
ginger *14*
grapefruit *13, 109*
grapes *13, 116*

H
haddock *52, 119*
hair *105, 152–67, 187*
hazelnuts *17, 18*
healthy diet *5, 8–11, 118–35*
heart *22, 23, 46–67, 186*
herbs, measurements *19*
honey *17*

I
immune system *22, 24–42, 186*
ingredients *9, 18*

J
joint problems *22, 23, 86–103, 186*

K
kidneys *15, 54*
kiwifruit *13, 64, 70, 109*

L
lamb *15, 74, 120*
leeks *48, 126, 132*
lemons *13, 52, 64, 90, 141, 158*
lentils *16, 58*
limes *13, 52*
linseeds *11, 17*
liver *15, 76, 93, 159, 175*

M
macadamia nuts *17*
mackerel *72, 172*
mangoes *13, 94, 106, 116*
mayonnaise *18, 20*
measurements *19*
meat and poultry
  nutritional benefits *15*
meat and poultry dishes
  braised lamb's liver with apples *159*
  chicken and broccoli pasta bake *176*
  chicken and mixed pepper stir-fry *56*
  chicken and wild mushroom risotto *160*
  chinese style roast lemon chicken *141*
  country chicken and barley casserole *76*
  devilled kidneys *54*
  grilled lamb cutlets with plum tomato salsa *120*
  Italian chicken casserole *118*
  lamb and apricot pilaf *74*
  lamb's liver with Madeira sauce *175*
  lemon chicken kebabs with herbed rice *52*
  oven-baked turkey with mango salsa *94*
  pan-fried liver with mushrooms and sage *76*
  sweet and sour turkey meatballs *54*
  turkey and brussels sprouts stir-fry *142*
melon *12, 70, 116, 154*
menus *44–5, 66–7, 84–5, 102–3, 150–1, 166–7, 184–5*
microwaving *18*
millet *15*
minerals *8, 22, 188–90*

N
nails *105, 136–51, 187*
nectarines *13, 148*
nuts *10, 16–17, 35, 42, 145, 165*

O
oats *15–16, 40, 165, 182*
oils, nutritional benefits *17, 18*
oily fish *10, 15*
onions *14, 60, 112*
oranges *13, 109*

P
pancakes, buckwheat *98*
papayas (pawpaw) *9, 13*
parsley *14*
pasta *16, 58, 136, 176*
peaches *13, 116*
peas *16, 112*
peppers see *sweet peppers*
pineapples *9, 13*
potatoes *15, 126, 136*, see *also sweet potatoes*
poultry see meat and poultry
prawns *30, 92, 154*
protein *10, 118–23*
pulses *16*
pumpkin
  nutritional benefits *15*
  seeds *11, 17, 36*

R

raspberries *13, 40, 82, 100, 116*
refined foods *8, 9*
rice, brown *16, 32, 72, 74, 124, 143, 160*
rye

S

salads
  char-grilled vegetable *114*
  dressings *11, 21*
  fruit and nut coleslaw *33*
  fruit and nut rice *143*
  mixed leaf and herb, with haloumi *168*
  shredded beetroot and carrot *138*
  spinach and avocado *154*
  sweet pepper, tomato and basil *26*
  tomato and broad bean couscous *128*
  warm seafood with fresh herbs *28*
salmon *15, 30, 72, 136*
salt *11, 18*
sardines *13, 140*
seafood, *see also fish*
  brochettes *88*
  crab-stuffed avocado *48*
  nutritional benefits *13*
  prawn and broccoli stir-fry *92*
  squid with chilli sauce *174*
  thai-spiced tiger prawns with tomato salsa *30*
  warm seafood salad with fresh herbs *28*
seeds *11, 17*
sesame seeds *11, 17, 18, 178*
skin *10, 104–5, 136–31, 187*
soups and starters
  asparagus and broccoli scramble *46*
  beetroot and carrot salad *138*
  Brussels sprouts and leek soup *48*
  carrot and barley soup *152*
  carrot and coriander soup *24*
  chunky vegetable soup *110*
  crab-stuffed avocado *48*
  cucumber and mint soup *113*
  green vegetable frittata *88*
  melon and kiwifruit cocktail *70*
  melon and prawn starter *134*
  mixed leaf and herb salad with haloumi *168*
  mushroom and asparagus frittata *170*
  pea and onion soup *112*
  red pepper soup *86*
  roasted baby vegetables *68*
  seafood brochettes *88*
  spinach and avocado salad *154*
  spinach soufflé *70*
  sweet pepper, tomato and basil salad *26*
  sweet peppers with goat's cheese *26*
  watercress soup *136*
soy sauce *18*
soya beans *10, 16, see also tofu*
spinach *13, 70, 154, 168*
star fruit *12*
starch-based meals *124–9*
starters see *soups and starters*
steaming *18*
stock *13, 20*
strawberries *13, 40, 64, 82, 100, 109*
sugars *8, 9–10, 17, 18*
sunflower seeds *11, 17, 18*
sweet peppers *14, 26, 36, 60, 86, 124*
sweet potatoes *13, 144, 178*

T

teeth and bones *68–87, 186*
tofu *16, 78, 162*
tomatoes *13, 26, 30, 120, 128*
toxins, elimination of *9, 104, 106–17*
trout *90, 138*
tuna *122*
turkey *34, 94, 142*

V

vegetable dishes
  bean goulash *180*
  bean and vegetable chilli *96*
  carrot, courgette and broccoli stir-fry *130*
  char-grilled vegetable salad *114*
  chunky vegetable soup *110*
  curry *134*
  fruit and nut coleslaw *33*
  fruit and nut rice salad *143*
  green vegetable frittata *88*
  green vegetable stir-fry with pumpkin seeds *36*
  oven-baked compote *132*
  pasta primavera *38*
  peppers stuffed with herbed rice *124*
  potato, leek and coriander rösti *126*
  roast vegetables with garlic and herbs *129*
  roast sweet potatoes *144*
  roasted baby vegetables *68*
  root vegetable and lentil stew *38*
  spiced couscous *78*
  spicy root vegetables *60*
  stock *20*
  summer vegetable quiche *96*
  sweet potato wedges with sesame seeds *178*
  tofu and carrot burgers *162*
  tofu and vegetable kebabs *78*
  tomato and broad bean couscous salad *128*
vegetables
  in diet *9, 11*
  green *14, 36, 88*
  nutritional benefits *13–15*
  protein *10*
  root *13, 38, 60*
vitamins *8, 9, 22, 188–9*

W

walnuts *17, 18*
water *8, 11*
watercress *13, 136, 168*
wheat *10, 18*
wholegrains *8, 9, 16, 18*

Y

yoghurt *16, 82, 100, 108, 182*

acknowledgements

Grateful thanks to Dr Udo Erasmus from Canada for his facts on essential fats, and in the UK, the Institute of Optimum Nutrition and Patrick Holford, and nutritionist Gareth Zeal for their support. Thanks also to my co-author Kathryn Marsden for being a true friend.

Hazel Courteney

Many people have worked very hard to prepare this book. My respect and admiration must go, in particular, to Hazel Courteney, and to Anne Sheasby who created the sumptuous store of recipes. It has been a pleasure to work with such conscientious and caring professionals.

Kathryn Marsden

I would like to thank Robert for his on-going support and encouragement with this book and for his tireless tasting of all the recipes; Kathryn Marsden for all her help and advice; Anne Townley and Viv Croot for asking me to create all the recipes for this book; and Molly Perham and Caroline Earle for all their hard editing work.

Anne Sheasby